UNSTOPPABLE
SUCCESS

*A Proven System
for Reaching the*
TOP 1% *in*
Everything You Do

Mike Mason

T0106749

UNSTOPPABLE SUCCESS
A Proven System for Reaching the TOP 1% *in Everything You Do*

by **Mike Mason**
© 2012 Mike Mason. All rights reserved.

ISBN 978-1-61448-097-6 Paperback
ISBN 978-1-61448-098-3 eBook
Library of Congress Control Number: 2011937673

Published by:
MORGAN JAMES PUBLISHING
The Entrepreneurial Publisher
5 Penn Plaza, 23rd Floor
New York City, New York 10001
(212) 655-5470 Office
(516) 908-4496 Fax
www.MorganJamesPublishing.com

Cover Design by:
Rachel Lopez
rachel@r2cdesign.com

Interior Design by:
Bonnie Bushman
bbushman@bresnan.net

In an effort to support local communities, raise awareness and funds, Morgan James Publishing donates one percent of all book sales for the life of each book to Habitat for Humanity.
Get involved today, visit
www.HelpHabitatForHumanity.org.

THIS BOOK IS DEDICATED TO

My wife, Natalie, for being a constant source of love, support and motivation.

My parents, Bill and Linda, for teaching me that anything is possible.

My family and friends for inspiring me to dream bigger and become more.

My sports and business coaches for pushing me to be my best so that I can help others be their best as well.

To my children, Rachel and Tyler. May your lives be amazing, may your dreams be inspiring, and may you be *unstoppable* in reaching your goals and achieving your purpose.

TABLE OF CONTENTS

INTRODUCTION

You are greater than you realize. You are meant to *be* more. You are meant to *do* more. You are meant to *have* more. You are capable of so much more.

In the pages of this book, you will find life lessons and examples from a variety of sources that will help you to develop a life of endless motivation. If you are interested in being the best of the best in all that you do, this book will show you how. I've personally used the principles that you will be learning to help me reach the top 1 percent in everything from athletics and academics to entrepreneurship. These strategies have worked for me, and they will work for you too. I've had the good fortunate to be around some of the most incredible people in the world in their respective professions, and I have identified several common traits that are consistently present in those who accomplish the most in life. I have included stories about many of them that showcase these particular traits in ways that will inspire you to follow in their footsteps. Once you see that there is very little difference between them and you, you will feel compelled to take your life to the next level. As the saying goes, success is not for the chosen few, but rather for the few who choose.

It has always intrigued me that so many people seem to go through life unhappy with their circumstances, not realizing that true happiness and the achievement of every single one of their goals or wants are within their grasp… and a lot closer than they think. By the end of this book, my hope is that you will have changed the way you are currently thinking by raising your expectations for every aspect of your life. I want you to *choose* to live a motivated life. And once you have chosen to change the way you think, you will begin to do what you are capable of doing each and every day and living as you were meant to live.

Life was *not* intended to be an unpleasant experience for you. God created each one of us for greatness. So whether you are unhappy with your current place in life or simply want to take your success to the next level, this book is for you. I will provide you with a system that will challenge you to dream bigger—and that will help to add more sanity and perspective to your life in the process. You will receive insight into defining and managing your priorities on a daily basis, while raising the bar on your personal expectations. This book has been ten years in the making, and will provide you with a step-by-step plan for building a larger, more balanced life.

As I become your coach through the following pages, I want you to know that I truly care about your success. I want to teach you to have everything you want in life and to give everything you have to it. In that sense, I'm passing on the help that my own mentors gave me. For example, the greatest coach and teacher I have ever had was my college wrestling coach and now pastor, Reverend Nate Carr. Nate was a three-time NCAA champion in college and a member of the 1988 Olympic team in Seoul, Korea, where he earned a bronze medal.

As I entered the collegiate wresting program at West Virginia University, Nate told me, "Mike, I have achieved great things in the sport of wrestling and in life. My championships have already been won. My awards have already been given to me. I have already been to the top of the mountain. My goal and purpose behind pushing you hard as my student has nothing to do with me… it's all about you. Unless you stand on the top of the podium as the greatest wrestler in the United States, you'll never know what it feels like to be there. Do what I tell you to do, and you'll give yourself the best opportunity of experiencing it for yourself. So even when times are tough and you don't necessarily feel like following through, remember that my coaching is for you, not for me. I want you to experience everything that I have been fortunate enough to experience myself."

I now tell *you* the same thing. I want you to experience the joy that I feel every single moment of my life. I want you to *be* the person that you were meant to be, to *do* what you were intended to do, and to *have* all that you were meant to have. I have been blessed with so much that I feel it is my duty and *purpose* to now share the approach that led to my accomplishments, so that you too can be motivated for life. If you follow every suggestion that I give you, you will see for yourself how easy it truly is to be successful at anything you choose, and you will be on your way to living the life of your dreams.

Why should you listen to me?

Anytime I read a new book or attend a new conference, I first want to confirm that the authors or teachers have actually done what they are proposing. I can assure you that I have done every single thing that I recommend to you in this book and have been successful with it. Are there other ways to get motivated? Of course! Do these other ways work for other people? Of course! But I'm not writing about those other methods, because I haven't done them *myself*. Rest assured that the examples of motivation that I will give you in the upcoming pages have been integral in shaping how I see my motivated life, and how I ultimately developed my own motivational routine.

Another reason to follow my system is that I am ordinary in every sense of the word, but I have been able to achieve some amazing things, despite being neither extraordinary nor having any amazing intellectual or physical gifts. I have been successful in sports, in academics, in coaching, in business, and in life. I have done these things with *motivation* as the backbone of my accomplishments. I am motivated to achieve despite my shortcomings. And because I am motivated, it carries me beyond my physical, intellectual, and emotional limitations. I truly believe that nothing is impossible for me, and by the end of this book, my goal is for you to believe that *nothing* is impossible for you!

How to Read This Book

The book is arranged to first teach you how motivated people *think*. As you progress through the pages, you will be asked to write down a few statements. Go out and buy a simple three-ring binder and keep everything you write down in this binder; it will become your "Motivational Binder," which I'll refer to throughout. We'll go over it again toward the end of the book. I want you to commit right now to actually doing what I ask you to do in the order I ask you to do it. In that way, I'll teach you how to duplicate the exact plan that has led me and others to phenomenal success.

Ultimately, you will develop a plan to get and stay *internally* motivated. I firmly believe that no one can acquire nor maintain motivation in the long-term unless they do it themselves. That's why I want you to follow my system, because when you do, you will find ways to tap into and develop your own individual, internal motivational system by finding your own purpose. You will find that, just like your new, motivated life, the lessons you learn in this book will gain momentum as they progress, and the practical applications toward the end of our journey will be worth the wait. Motivated people always finish what they start. Commit right now to actually reading through this entire book. If you can do that, I can assure you that your life will be changed.

I am committed to *your* success! It is part of my purpose in life to help you reach your goals. So let's start our journey and get inspired this second to lead a greater life than the one you've had up to this point. Get ready, because... the bar is going up!

> *You can get everything in life that you want... if you'll just*
> *help enough other people get what they want.* —Zig Ziglar

Chapter 1

THE BEGINNING OF WINNING

In case you haven't noticed, time moves quickly. My goal is to give you all the tools you need to start getting motivated for life *today*! You never know what tomorrow may hold. How many times have you seen someone on television who went through tragedy but is now doing extraordinary things? Lance Armstrong was given a second chance at life and became more motivated than ever to reach his potential. Countless successful athletes, businessmen, and Hollywood superstars survive tragedies, either in their own lives or the lives of loved ones, only to take their careers and spiritual lives to a whole new level.

If you have been through one of these events and are now working to make the most of things by getting motivated to reach your full potential, I commend you. Know that this book will help take you to the next level.

However, if you have not been through anything tragic yet, let me walk you through the implications of the following realization: life is going to end for us and for our family members and friends. Some of us will receive notice that it's going to happen, and some of us won't. Some of us will be given a second chance, and some of us won't. Motivation begins with the realization that life will one day come to an end. You don't have all the time in the world! I want this book to motivate you to make life everything that you can possibly make it *today*.

It's On You

You don't have to wait for something terrible to happen before you become motivated to be the best you that you can be. I've seen athletes who have wasted their careers and never achieved success because they were not motivated. I've seen talented students fail out of school because they were not motivated. I've seen people's health fade away early because they were not motivated. I've seen religious people go through life spiritually unhappy because they were not motivated. All of these people knew what they needed to do, but none of them did anything about it…until it was too late. I have seen all of these people on a daily basis for years now, and they all have one thing in common. They all eventually get to a point where they regret not doing what they knew they should do. But not you! Not now! I'm going to give you advice and instructions on how to achieve your potential *today*. If you are willing to consistently use the tools that I will give you, you'll find that getting motivated to achieve any result you choose will become much easier than it has been in the past.

Nothing in the world can take the place of persistence. Talent will not; nothing is more common than unsuccessful men with talent. Genius will not; the world is full of educated derelicts. Persistence and determination alone are omnipotent. The slogan 'press on' has solved and always will solve the problems of the human race.
—Calvin Coolidge

You can *be, do,* and *have* everything you want if you are motivated *today* to make it happen. The bad news is also the good news…It's on you. No one can make these things happen for you but *you*. This book will guide you through a simple process to both get and keep yourself motivated to take action, but ultimately, it is your responsibility to put these suggestions to work right now. If you follow my advice, you'll learn what I have found to be a simple formula for success through daily motivation.

Let me start by saying you need this book because everyone needs to have a system in place in order to get and stay motivated. Very few people are motivated to be their best, and all of us need to be coached and challenged if we are going to stretch our vision of what is possible.

Here's a simple example that proves my point:

For years now, when coaching athletes, I've commonly used the phrase "It's on you." For example, I often end our practices with conditioning work by lining the teams up to run sprints, and I inevitably ask the question, "Who wants it? Who wants to guarantee me that they'll win the next race?" If someone takes my challenge, they must win the race, or else they're forced to run an additional sprint while the rest of the team rests and watches. If they win the race, they get to rest and watch while the rest of the team does an extra sprint. The fun part is getting to a point where no one takes my challenge. I then pick someone out of the crowd that has not had the responsibility of winning yet. Often, it's someone from the middle or the back of the pack.

When I point to that person and say, "It's on you," something magical happens. Nine times out of ten, that person is the one who wins the next race. All they needed was for one person to give them the responsibility of performing at a higher level. All they needed was for a coach to believe in them. All they needed was the motivation to be their best. And nearly every time, that alone will put them ahead of everyone else. My goal in saying, "It's on you" is not necessarily to get you to be the best at everything you do, but rather to be *your* best.

That is my purpose in writing this book. I want to call you out and say, "It's on you!" Whatever it is that you were meant to *be, do,* and *have* is available to you already. My goal is to get you to take action and get motivated and excited to make it happen today. I thank you for letting me be your coach and for letting me help you reach your potential. This is going to be fun, and you are going to be awesome.

You Are Worth the Effort

One of the first aspects of living a truly motivated life lies in the realization that you are worth it. You deserve to have, be, and do everything in this lifetime that you are capable of achieving. A motivated life is available to anyone and everyone who is ready *today* to get the most out of life and give the most to life every second. Each of us has our own specific capabilities. Each of us has our own specific desires. Each of us has our own specific ideas of what living a motivated life looks like. There's enough opportunity for every single one of us to have everything that we want to have, to be everything that we want to be, and to do everything that we want to do. God did not give us all of these abilities in the hopes that we would not use our gifts. You were not given extraordinary potential at birth with a disclaimer that stated, "Please keep these abilities a secret" attached to you. You were meant for greatness. However, these gifts were given to you along with the choice of using them to maximize your potential...or not.

According to Rick Warren, author of *The Purpose Driven Life,* one of the two questions that you will be asked by God when you die is "What did you do with what I gave you?" Notice the question is *not* "What did you *think* about what I gave you?" or "Did I give you anything?" We all have gifts. Spectacular gifts! Gifts that, if used, will yield more than you ever dreamed. God has every intention for you to use your gifts to live a motivated life. A life in which every moment is spent both getting and giving everything possible. Remember, the question is "What did you *do* with what I gave you?" (As a side note, if you have never read Rick Warren's *The Purpose Driven Life,* I strongly urge you to do so. I promise you it will be worth your time.)

I often refer to the biblical quote "To whom much has been given, much is required" (Luke 12:48). Think of all the blessings that are yours to enjoy right now. Think about all of the special people who have come into your life at one time or another. Think about all of the abilities that you have been given. God gave each of us the capacity to *be, do,* and *have* more than our feeble minds will often allow us to believe. You have been given everything you need to live a motivated life right now—right this second!

If we can agree that you have been given everything that you need to be the ultimate *you*, then let's focus on the second half of the quote, "much is required." Those who have the ability to *be, do,* and *have* more in this life also have the responsibility to achieve their potential. It's less about what you have been given, and more about what you do with it. I have never been, nor do I claim to be, extraordinary at any particular aspect of life. But I have achieved, and continue to achieve, great things simply because I do as much as possible with every gift that I have been given. At the same time, I still see more potential in my own life each and every day. By seeing my gifts, I am driven to live a motivated life today. And by seeing my potential, I am driven to be even more motivated tomorrow.

So as we go through the process of achieving and living a life that is motivated, remember that the key word is *do*. You can only create a motivated life of your own if you *implement* the lessons you read here. Knowledge is power, but it is what you do with that knowledge that will take you to the life of your dreams.

To know and not to do is not yet to know. —Zen Koan

Success Strategies

- There is enough opportunity for every single person to *have, be,* and *do* whatever it is they want.

- God intends you to use your gifts to achieve success.

- Those who have the ability to *be, do,* and *have* more also have the *responsibility* to *be, do,* and *have* more.

- Knowledge is power, but what you do with that knowledge is equally important.

Attitude

So, now that you know you are worth the effort, it's time to adjust your attitude. That's because attitude is everything. It's the only way you can raise the level of your life in all areas. As an athletic coach, for several years I have begun each season with a quote from John Maxwell:

"Your attitude at the beginning of a task will affect the outcome more than anything else." As a business owner, I have begun each new staff member's employment the same way. As a coaching client myself, I begin each task, event, or goal by revisiting this quote and making sure that my own attitude is in check. Nothing will tell you more about what to expect from someone's future than their attitude. If the attitude is right, nothing will be impossible. And I mean absolutely *nothing*!

Are you honestly living up to your potential? I venture to say that you could be doing better; we all could. A likely cause of your inability to lead the life that you've always dreamed of is your attitude. So let's have an attitude check right now.

As you go through the following questions, answer them honestly. Record the answers in your Motivational Binder. After answering them, review the ones that need work and highlight the ones that you want to focus on the most. I urge you to come back to them later on for a follow-up to assess the improvements that you've made. Regardless of where you begin, if you follow the steps outlined ahead and learn from each of the lessons, you will be amazed at how much change can be made in your attitude and your life in a short time. Changing your attitude will be another giant step toward doing what those who are motivated for life do to achieve success.

Questions for your Motivational Binder

- Are you living at the level that you could be?

- Are you excited about changing your life for the better, or are you just reading another book, going through the motions, and *trying* to do better?

- Are you following your priorities each day and keeping first things first?

- Are you excited when you wake up in the morning, ready to make the most of another day?

- Are you working as smart and as hard as you can?

- Are you doing what you know you should be doing?
- Are you motivated for life each and every day?

If your answer was no to any one of these questions, don't be alarmed, because you're not alone. It'll be easy to answer *yes!* to all these questions after you work on...

Chapter 2

PLANNING SUCCESS

To paraphrase Blaise Pascal, "Most of life's problems come from man's inability to sit alone in a room for three hours." There are many ways that you could interpret this quote. The interpretation that I have settled on myself is that most people have not taken the time to actually think about what they want and establish their purpose. To live a motivated life, you need to have direction. To have direction, you must have a destination. In order to find your destination, you must have purpose.

Finding Your Purpose

Most people, when either asked about what they want in life or asked about their purpose in life, do not have an answer. It has been my experience that most people simply have not taken the time out of their busy schedules to sit alone in a quiet room until they determine where they are going and the purpose behind their mission. Most people simply complain. They complain about their jobs. They complain about the economy. They complain about their friends. They complain about their family. They complain about their lives! Ask these same people what they *want* in their lives, and they can't tell you. It's hard to actually get what you want if you don't know what that is. It's hard to create a motivated life if you don't have a vision of what your motivated life would look like. It's even harder to have a truly motivated life if you have no purpose behind your vision.

So, let's work on the most difficult part of this equation: your purpose.

First, let me provide my own purpose as an example. My personal mission is this: "To lead others to health, wealth, and better lives by helping people realize their own potential, while at the same time, living up to my own."

After defining my purpose, I've been able to dream bigger and aim for much higher goals. Additionally, through knowing my purpose, I've been able to maintain a consistent personal mission that has driven me to stay motivated. In sum, this purpose has given me my "why" in life.

Without your "why," it will be easy to give up on your goals. It will be easy to settle for less. It will be easy to quit. But once you establish your life's purpose, you will be on your way to a motivated life. Once you've defined your purpose, you know where you are going. It is much easier to plan a path to *somewhere* than it is to *nowhere*. By defining your purpose, you are putting the end at the beginning. One of my best friends and personal coaches preaches that you must always "speak the end of a thing at the beginning." You must know where you are going. After taking the time to sit alone in a room and establish your purpose, you'll be able to speak your end at your beginning.

The secret to success is the constancy of purpose. —Keith Maule

At this point, I want you to add a critical component to your personalized Motivational Binder. The statement of your purpose is the *most important* part of this crucial motivational tool, which you will have completed by the end of this book. To print your *free*, easy-to-download "Purpose Statement form," visit www.unstoppablesuccess.com and click on "Free Gift."

To once again reference *The Purpose Driven Life*, the opening line states, "It's not about you."[1] This one line truly defines what I believe to be

1   Rick Warren, The Purpose Driven Life, 17.

both the problem and solution to most people's lack of motivation. Most people's daily objectives revolve around themselves. It's human nature. Two things that people are constantly struggling for are money and time. Think about it. Most of our days are spent working to make more money in the shortest amount of time possible. When you complain about things in your life to your friends and family, think about how many of those complaints come back to those two fundamentals of money and time. The problem is that when we are working for these two things with a selfish purpose, we become immediately greedy with them both. Suddenly, the money we're trying to make just isn't worth it anymore, because we just don't have enough time. When we do have time to enjoy life, we don't want to spend our money, because it took so much of our time to make it. However, if you are working for reasons outside of yourself, you no longer become greedy about these two things.

Life is not about what you have, but what you have to give.
—Oprah Winfrey

If you have a purpose outside of yourself, suddenly you see your own ability to give your time and money. It is much easier to live a motivated life when your purpose and your goals are geared toward others. The key lies in establishing a purpose that is not centered around you. However, this purpose will help to keep you motivated to be your best in every aspect of life if you follow it.

I truly believe that the best way to keep yourself motivated on a daily basis is to place the importance of being motivated on something or someone *other* than you. My sister's experience as a student is a perfect example. Growing up, she had to work extremely hard in school just to keep up. Most people in grade school simply get up, go to school, learn the material, maybe (or maybe not) do a little homework, take a test, and earn a decent grade. This was not the case for my sister. She was gifted in many areas of life, but learning new material in order to take tests was a very big challenge for her. She had to put in much more time than the average person in the evening to achieve mediocre grades. I remember many times waking up to get ready for class, only to see her at the end of an hour-long study session before going to school. She struggled, but always put in the necessary effort to do her best.

As fate would have it, she faced a very big assignment when she was in the fifth grade, in which the teacher told the class that they would be partnered up for a team project. They would be jointly evaluated and given a common grade based on their partnership's competence. Her best friend growing up was a 4.0 student and had never earned a grade other than an A in her life. Since the two sat together in class, they were paired up. That evening, it must have sunk in for my sister that her best friend's academic record rested on her shoulders. She began working and studying immediately. She recruited me as an audience, and I can remember listening while she recited her portion of the project to me exhaustively. Over and over and over, she recited her portion of the information until she could do it in her sleep. When the day to finally deliver came around, sure enough, she nailed it. She recited the information just as she'd practiced all those times in her room. And the grade she received? An A+.

Now, if you'd asked my sister before this project if she was working as hard as she possibly could to excel in the classroom, she would have said yes. However, when her purpose for studying was centered on someone other than herself, she discovered another, dormant level that had never been touched. Had the same project been given on an individual basis, her efforts would have been the same as always, and she would have gotten what she always got: Bs and Cs. But when her purpose was to help maintain her best friend's perfect 4.0, her motivation went to a previously untouched level.

As you begin to develop your own Purpose Statement, use the following list of examples as a guide to help you find one that is centered around other people.

- The students motivated to make good grades to make their parents proud…

- The athletes motivated to perform well for their coaches and team…

- The mothers motivated to provide the best for their children...
- The fathers motivated to provide for their families...
- The coaches motivated to get the most from athletes for their own success...
- The business owners motivated to provide the best for their clients and staff...
- The employees motivated to achieve their objectives and pursue the company mission...
- The politicians motivated to serve the people's interest...
- The attorneys motivated to protect their clients' interests...
- The healthcare providers motivated to help their patients gain and maintain optimum health...

All these people will remain more motivated and will be more successful than anyone selfishly motivated by an undefined or self-serving purpose.

This aspect of establishing our purpose is essential in living a motivated life. As you assemble your Motivational Binder, which will be the cornerstone of your own motivated life, your written Purpose Statement will be placed as page number one in the binder. It is the most important motivational tool that you will ever have. Revisit your Purpose Statement and make sure that it revolves around people, groups, or things other than yourself if you want to obtain your highest level of motivation.

Success Strategies

- Establish a purpose for your life that revolves around someone or something other than yourself.
- A selfless purpose will allow you to give freely of your time and your money.
- In order to succeed, you must know what you want.

- A selfless purpose is the first step toward achieving the top 1 percent in all that you do.

- Visit www.unstoppablesuccess.com and click on "Free Gift" to download a printable version of your Purpose Statement form, to be used in your Motivational Binder.

- Once you establish the purpose behind your goals, review it daily to become unstoppable.

If you still need convincing that your life will get better when you focus on others rather than yourself, then it's time to play the game called...

20–5–1

A few years ago, I went through a yearlong program called "The Big Table," taught and led by Loral Langemeier, author of several books, most notably *The Millionaire Maker*. The program was a very good investment, and one that I would advise you to pursue. While the program was extremely beneficial, many of the lessons that I came away with were more about life and helping others than about money and finances.

After the initial seminar, we were placed in five- to seven-person "Mastermind Groups." (By the way, the mastermind principle is clearly defined in the timeless *Think and Grow Rich* by Napoleon Hill. If you have never been a part of such a group, I urge you to read the book and start your own group as soon as possible.) These groups were to remain the same until our following seminar four months later. Periodically, we met in person or by telephone to discuss and brainstorm ideas that would help each us to reach our goals. As it happened, in our group, the primary focus was on our various businesses, and we met weekly to discuss any ideas that other members might have about resolving specific issues that had taken place during the week. Each week, when we showed up, we had a specific amount of time to focus on each person in the group, during which other members would offer advice to their present challenges.

It was fascinating to both give and receive advice from other people in various parts of the country in completely unrelated businesses. The advice that I received allowed my businesses to grow by leaps and bounds in the course of our time together. Upon learning more about each of the businesses, I found myself spending time during the week, in between calls, researching information and planning ideas to give to the members at the following meeting. In return, I received much-needed insight into my own business each week during the phone calls, so I made it my goal to make sure that I spent the proper time each week preparing to help the other team members reach their goals. I pulled information from the Internet for other members of my group, sent them books, passed on information from other business seminars that I thought would be useful to them in their particular business, and made several calls to individuals in between mastermind calls, when I came up with ideas for them that I needed more time to discuss. My primary drive became to help them reach all of their individual goals by the time that we were to switch groups four months later.

Upon returning to the second seminar, Loral instructed each of us to return from lunch with a $20 bill, a $5 bill, and a $1 bill, but did not tell us why. After lunch, we were seated in a large circle around the room and given three Post-its on which to write. Our first instruction was to write down the name of the person who had helped us the most during that four-month time frame, and why we were thankful for their help. After doing so, we were instructed to attach the Post-it to the $20 bill and give it to that person. Next, we did the same thing with the second-most helpful person and attached the $5 bill. Finally, we wrote the name of the third-most influential person on the last Post-it, attached it to the $1 bill, and gave it to that person.

After we had completed this task, we then were organized by the amount of money in our hands following the exchange, from largest amount to smallest, and once again re-formed in a circle. As I looked around the room, only about half of the sixty people had any money at all. Again, there were five to seven people in each group, yet we only had three bills to give away, so each of us could not possibly give a bill to *everyone* else in our group; we only had enough for the top three.

Here's where the lesson came in. When lined up from the most money to the least, I ended in the fifth chair out of the sixty people. As I looked across the room, I saw one of my team members beginning to tear up. When I looked in her hands, she had no money. Every week during our conference calls, she'd had a new personal crisis to discuss. She spent all of her allotted time complaining about one thing or another, and the rest of the group worked diligently to bring her spirits up. Yet, when each of the other people had their turn to speak and ask for help, she had nothing to offer. She was happy to get our input, yet was nowhere to be found when someone else needed her help. Maybe she felt like she had nothing to give. Maybe she felt like her advice would not be good enough. Maybe she felt like it was not her place to give advice. Regardless, because of her selfish approach to the group, she was left sitting with tears in her eyes and no money in her hands.

In contrast, the person sitting in the lead chair at the end of the game had over $120 in her hands. She'd had only $26 to give, and ended up with over *four* times that amount. She is the one we should all be working to emulate. Not only did she help her own team members accomplish their four-month goals, but she also went outside of her group to help other groups as well. Again, no one knew that we would be playing this game at the following seminar, so her actions were for the sole purpose of helping others. And unlike the other people left holding *some* money like me, she was left holding a *lot* of money. Why? Because she helped more people than we did.

Like her, I had not intended to get anything in return for the help I had given the other people in our group. I had gone into the four-month stint with the goal of helping every one of my team members achieve their goals, yet when all was said and done, I was the one holding most of the money from our group. When the purpose behind your actions is to help others get what they want and need, you'll always receive more for yourself in the end. Whatever it is that you hope to accomplish, make your focus and purpose one that benefits *others*. The rewards that you will receive will be beyond what you will ever give.

The lessons here apply not only to finances and business, but also to every other facet of life. The real joy and the real reward lies in helping others get what they want. Only when your day begins and ends with others in mind will you live at your potential. Even the most minor events in your life can lead to amazing payoffs when they are performed with others in mind.

Success Strategies

- Mastermind groups are an effective way to reach greater levels of success.

- Be willing to give freely of knowledge and skills and willingly accept help from others.

- When your purpose is to help others, you will always receive more than you give in return.

- To increase your success, find more ways to help more people.

- Only when you begin and end each day with others in mind will you reach your full potential.

These principles were also proven true in my trip to....

Palm Springs

I traveled to Palm Springs a few years ago to attend a special conference for a business-coaching program I was completing. These conferences are only available to those businesses that have reached a certain level of success, and are always held at very nice places. This resort was no exception; in fact, it was so luxurious that it came as no surprise that several famous politicians were present for their own conference the same weekend that we were there. Everything—the rooms, the amenities, the pools, the spa, and the décor—was the best of the best. The conference itself was held in a very plush suite with a beautiful view of the main pool, and a clear view of the private golf course. Needless to say, it was a challenge to fully focus on the conference, given the magnificence of our surroundings.

As is typical of these conferences, the exact agenda was somewhat of a mystery until it actually began. Serendipitously enough, the training agenda for the weekend was based around staffing. This came at a crucial time for me, as I had begun to face staffing challenges during the few weeks leading up to the conference. While all of the conference attendees discussed staffing solutions, bonus systems, training, etc., I listened intently to their ideas and attempted to plan an approach for successfully dealing with my own staffing issues at home. The CEO of the management company that ran the conference also offered his advice in dealing with various staff issues. By the end of the conference, I had several ideas on how to deal with these challenges, but was still a little unsure about how to approach each issue. My plan was to spend the entire return trip refining the various ideas that I had acquired at the conference into a solid plan to implement once I returned.

After leaving the resort to return to the Palm Springs Airport, I sat in the very small terminal there and quickly scribbled down staffing plans. Unfortunately, the more I reviewed the discussions about staffing at the conference, the more upset I became about my particular issues. In retrospect, many of the plans that I was scribbling down in that airport terminal were not very constructive. After several minutes of frantic writing and typing, I decided to take a quick break and get myself a drink from the vending machine. As I was getting my water, a man walked up behind me to get in line. The man was dressed casually, with thick glasses and a belly that bulged slightly over his belt. As I reached for my drink, the man asked, "Does this machine only take one-dollar bills?" I looked in his hand and saw that he was holding a twenty-dollar bill. As we both scoured over the sides of the machine, we noticed a sign printed in bold lettering: "Accepts $1 only." I quickly popped three one-dollar bills into the machine and asked the man what he was drinking.

He said, "I'll just have a water, please." I pressed the button to order a water and began walking back to my seat in the terminal. As I walked away, the man said, "Please, let me pay for it. Can you make change for a twenty?" I told him that I couldn't make change and not to worry about it. After I returned to my seat, the man approached me again. "Can I please make change and pay you back?" he asked.

"Really, it's no big deal. You're welcome," I replied.

The man continued, "Thank you so much! You know, people just don't seem to do nice things like that anymore. It means a lot that you'd spend money without wanting anything in return."

Again I replied, "You're welcome." As the man walked away, I thought to myself, *it was only three dollars. It wasn't that big of a deal. I wonder why three dollars meant a lot to him?*

About that time, our airplane began boarding. There were only fifteen to twenty people on the flight out of Palm Springs, and it was probably the smallest commercial plane on which I have ever traveled. As I got myself into my seat, moving my carry-on luggage under the seat, I looked up and saw the same gentleman boarding the plane. As he checked his ticket, he looked back in my direction. Where do you think his seat assignment was located? That's right, directly next to mine. As he sat down, he said, "Awesome, I get to sit next to the nice guy that spent money on a stranger!" Although I smiled, positive thoughts were not necessarily bouncing around inside my mind. To tell the truth, I thought his thanks were a bit too effusive. I began to read a book as the man continued to peek over my shoulder to see what I was reading. "I love that author," he said.

"Oh, you read his books too, do you?"

"Yeah, and I know him. We've done seminars together before." Now he had my attention, as this author is a very famous leadership figure, and based on what I've read, he speaks to thousands of people, but has a fairly small "inner circle." The gentleman went on to say, "So, is there anything that I can do for you? You were nice enough to buy me that water and wouldn't let me pay you back. What can I do for you?"

Again I replied, "Really, it's no big deal."

"What are you in town for?" he asked.

"I'm here for a business conference."

"Oh yeah? Where'd you stay?"

I told him where I had stayed and went on to explain, "If you've never been there, it's a must-see! It's one of the—if not *the*—nicest places I've ever stayed. Every single thing there was top-of-the-line. I can't wait to go back again someday."

"That makes me so happy to hear," he said. "That's one of my hotels."

That's right. That was one of his hotels! How the situation changed with that statement. This gentleman went from being someone who, in my mind, was hard-pressed for cash and annoyingly overly gracious about the three dollars that I had spent on his drink, to the CFO of one of the largest hotel chains in the world.

I closed my book, pulled out the notepad that I had taken for the conference, and turned myself sideways in my seat as an eager student ready to learn. Knowing exactly what had just happened, he again asked, "So, what can I do for you?"

I asked, "How many employees does your company have?" He stated the exact number that they currently employed, which was several thousand people. My request was then, "Will you tell me how you run your company as it relates to staffing?"

"Absolutely!" he replied.

For the next two hours, I got a behind-the-scenes look at a seven-billion-dollar company and how they handled staffing multiple hotels with employee numbering in the thousands. The seminar I had originally flown out for was extremely informative, but I learned as much, if not more, in the two hours with this complete stranger than I have at any conference or class I've ever attended. His solutions to my staffing issues transformed my business and set me on a much straighter path than my scribbled notes would have. And why did all of this happen? Because I spent three dollars on a bottle of water for this complete stranger and expected nothing in return.

The point is that the more you give, the more you get. Giving to people and expecting something in return is counterproductive and will only lead to disappointment, hurt feelings, and strained friendships. Give freely. Give to people who can never repay you. Give to those who can't do for themselves. Give your money, your time, your talents. When you give freely, it is amazing how all of it returns to you tenfold. God will send you what you need, when you need it, if you are only willing to be the person that you are supposed to be. A motivated life is a giving life.

Also, this is another reminder to treat everyone equally. That is, treat everyone as if he or she were the most important person in the world. You never know who you might be talking to, and the effect that your treatment will have on both them and you.

Success Strategies

- Give without expecting anything in return.
- Give freely of your money, your time, and your talents.
- The more you give, the more you get.
- A motivated life is a giving life.
- Treat everyone as if they are the most important person in the world.

Chapter 3

PRIORITIZING SUCCESS

Don't let the opinions of the average man sway you.
Dream and he thinks you're crazy. Succeed and he thinks
you're lucky. Acquire wealth and he thinks you're greedy. Pay
no attention. He simply doesn't understand. —Robert G. Allen

If you haven't noticed this already, much of the world does not think in a giving way. But starting now, you do! And because you do, you'll learn that you must occasionally say no to the people and things that don't match your purpose.

Choose to Say No!

While I believe there are no limitations to what I'm capable of achieving in this life, I have found that, in order to best serve my purpose, I must learn to say no to people and activities that do not support my goals. I have learned that I must go in the direction that's meant for me, regardless of where those around me would like to go. Once I determine that someone is not going in the same direction as I am, I no longer spend precious hours of my day with them. Once you define your purpose, your personal mission will provide direction for you. And once you know where you're going, identify the different people with whom you will surround yourself (see the "Rule of Three"). If the people with whom you surround yourself do not fall into one of those three categories, and they are not interested in moving in the same direction as you, surround yourself with people who are. Spending your time with people who lack a compatible life's purpose and who have no intention of helping you achieve yours is not the best way to spend your time. You must learn to say no to them.

Keep in mind that I'm not in any way suggesting that you shouldn't work as hard as possible to help those in need. I'm not saying that you should not befriend those who could benefit from your friendship. I'm simply saying that the majority of your time should be spent with those who support you and your personal mission. If you don't consciously decide who to spend your time with, you will inevitably be led astray by others who neither think nor act like you as you seek to achieve your motivated life.

You must also learn to say no to daily events and activities that do not support your purpose. I found this to be most important in my college days. I knew what I wanted from sports, I knew what I wanted from school, and I knew where I was going. If you attended college, or are currently attending, then you are familiar with the endless distractions campuses present. Upon my coach's recommendation, I wrote down my goals and my purpose on a note card and kept it in my wallet. I would read the note card several times each day. By continually reminding myself of my mission, I was able to avoid many of the distractions that keep college students from reaching their potential. I still carry these notes to remind me of my mission in life. Anytime that I find myself choosing whether or not to partake in activities, be they business related or otherwise (especially activities that will be more time-consuming), I look back at the Purpose Statement and goals and see if they match. If they do, I'm in! If not, I've learned that I *must* say no.

Again, I'm in no way saying that you can't enjoy life. I'm in no way saying that you shouldn't partake in fun activities simply for enjoyment. I'm simply saying that life will continue to throw excessive possibilities at you. You must prioritize your life, determine where you are going, and get involved in activities that allow you to work toward your mission.

It is essential that you review your Purpose Statement on a daily basis. If you don't, you'll quickly find yourself surrounded by people who don't support your mission. You'll find yourself in activities and daily events that do not bring you closer to achieving your purpose. Being motivated for life means that you'll work to be your best in all areas that you consider a priority, while saying *no* to people and things that do not bring you closer to your potential. Review your Purpose Statement often. Write it down, keep it with you at all times, and learn to say no when faced with options that do not coincide with what you have written.

As the saying goes, "You must have a yes to have a no." You must have a purpose with which to say yes to, so that you can say no to those people and things that do not match. Say yes to living a motivated life. Say yes to being your best at everything you do. Say yes to doing the things that you know you should do. Say yes to your priority list. Say yes to being all that you can be, doing all that you can do, and having all that you can have. Say no to distractions. Say no to paths that do not bring you closer to achieving your goals. Say no to people and things that steer you away from your purpose.

Success Strategies

- Surround yourself with people who support and encourage you.
- Say no to people who don't support your purpose.
- Say no to activities and events that don't support your purpose.
- Prioritize your life and get involved in activities that will take your toward your goals.
- Review your priorities daily and keep first things first.
- Ultimately, say no to living in the past and learn to…

Stop Relying On Yesterday's Success

You want to learn from your past, not live in it—
focus on the things that empower you. —Anthony Robbins

Another quality I have found to be consistent in virtually all-top achievers living a motivated life is their focus on the future. Simply put, they've learned to stop banking on yesterday's success. I have seen far too many people who have been successful in one aspect of life "decide" that they have reached the end. You are only as successful as you choose to be *today*. You have to give yourself daily motivation to keep from becoming complacent about your success. In my opinion, you must maintain two different activities that will drive you toward being your best *today* so that you can keep from becoming complacent. The first is consistently reviewing your purpose, goals, and priorities each and every day. The second is setting a goal and dream for your life that is truly beyond your reach.

The most successful athletes that I've ever met are continually striving to become better. A perfect example is a story that I heard at a wrestling camp when I was younger. Russ Helickson, longtime coach of the Ohio State Buckeyes, was a former wrestling powerhouse himself. In the early 1970s, he was a United States national champion, and earned the chance to compete overseas in the World Wrestling Tournament for a chance to claim the title of World Champion in his weight class. The tournament occurs only on years when the Olympic Games do not take place. Most of the top athletes treated the World Wrestling Tournament as an early preparation for the Olympic trials and Olympic Games.

In 1971, one year before the upcoming Olympic Games, Russ Helickson went to the World Wrestling Tournament. There, he was assigned a roommate by the name of Dan Gable, who had also earned a spot on the U.S. team in a different weight class. Russ and Dan had very different outcomes at the tournament. Russ did very well in the tournament, but did not achieve his goal of becoming a World Champion. However, Dan Gable was more successful, and ended the tournament on top of the podium as the World's Best Wrestler in his weight class.

While this was obviously a tremendous accomplishment, what happened the following day was something that Russ believed changed his life. As Russ told the story, most of the members of the United States team were "lying around feeling sorry for themselves, and even a little proud that they had gotten as far as they did." Upon awakening, Russ had noticed that his now World Champion roommate was nowhere to be found. About an hour later, Dan returned to the room sweating profusely, coming back from a long run. Here was a man who, just a day earlier, had achieved his goal of becoming a World Champion—and the very next morning; he was already working toward his next goal of becoming an Olympic champion! His long-term goal was large enough that he had no time to rest on his laurels after achieving success. He knew that a person is only as successful as he chooses to be *today*. Dan went on to win the 1972 Olympic Games, and is still considered one of the greatest athletes that the sport has ever known.

How many times have you seen former successful athletes who've chosen to not move on with their lives once their competition days have ended? Maybe *you* are one of these people. If so, you must remember that no one cares about what you did yesterday, and you shouldn't either. This doesn't mean that you shouldn't take pride in your accomplishments. It also doesn't mean that you shouldn't take time to celebrate every stepping-stone of achievement along your life's journey. And it certainly doesn't mean that you shouldn't use yesterday's successes and failures to help mold who you are today and who you're going to be tomorrow. What it *does* mean is that you must move on. There are bigger and better things to accomplish in your future. The most successful people in any endeavor understand that they must put their achievements to rest once they have been accomplished. You must have a long-term plan that forces you to immediately start working toward your next goal.

As Oprah Winfrey likes to repeat, whenever she's thought about retiring from her television show, her partner, Stedman Graham, has told her, "You'd better have a plan." He knows that, even with all of her career successes, she will not be happy unless she's working toward a future goal. Why? Because she's leading a motivated life; that's Oprah. If there's any businesswoman who has earned the right to live off of her past success, it's her. But one of the keys to her success is that, while she assuredly takes occasional glances backward at her former success, she is continually focused on a great today and an even better tomorrow.

One of my coaches always says, "You're not there yet!" I've found this to be absolutely true. No matter how big or how great your accomplishments, there's always more that you can achieve *today*. To live a motivated life, you need to make this idea a part of your plan. For my part, even though I've always considered myself a forward thinker, I still find this a challenge. I've been able to achieve some great things in life, but I've always worked to quickly move on to the next goal. However, even with that in mind, I continually find myself challenged to dream even bigger. As soon as I've put a one-year plan in place for my life, I meet someone who challenges me to develop a five-year plan. Once I complete a five-year plan, I meet someone who challenges me to develop a twenty-year plan. I've learned that I really am *not* there yet myself. In every aspect of my life, I've found at least one person, and most of the time many people, who are currently dreaming even bigger than I am. This has forced me to continually reevaluate my past successes with a new perspective. My accomplishments have merely been building blocks toward larger goals in my future. I have a lot of things still left to achieve. Knowing this, I've set goals that are beyond my ability to reach anytime soon. This keeps me motivated to stay on task and not relax.

Anytime you let up, expect a letdown. —John Maxwell

When it comes to yesterdays' successes in the workplace, the same principle holds true. Quite simply, your employer doesn't care about what you did yesterday. I've found that employees tend to frequently forget this fact. All businesses, and I mean all businesses, must have leaders who focus on *today's* accomplishments in order to create a better tomorrow for their businesses, their staff, and their clients. The fact that you may have been an essential part of the company's progress yesterday does *nothing* to help the business reach its future goals if you are not working to your capacity today. All too often, employees believe that a great day, great month, or even a great year somehow exempts them from further efforts. If your employer or manager is any good at all, they know what you are doing. More importantly, they know what you are *not* doing. Those who exceed management's expectations on a daily basis will never be overlooked for long. At the same time, there has been nothing more disappointing to me as an employer than a capable employee's unwillingness to do their best, or their reliance on what they did yesterday as a reason to keep them onboard. Additionally, I've seen applicants to my businesses whose only references were from several years ago, and often several jobs ago. This is an immediate red flag to me. These people are breaking the very rule that I'm writing about. They somehow think that the work they did for an employer ten years and six jobs ago is a good indication of what they can do to help my business. That past information may be a good indication of what they are *capable* of doing, but it's no indication of what they're willing to do *now*. If I cannot get the same kind of reference from their most recent employer, then I don't hire such applicants; they're relying too much on the past, and their sense of entitlement, based on long-ago successes, will not be a fit in my business.

The life you have led doesn't need to be the only life you have.
—Anna Quindlen

Success Strategies

- You are only as successful as you choose to be today.
- Consistently review your purpose, your priorities, and your goals each and every day.
- Have a long-term goal and dream for your life that will challenge you to let go of each small success so that you can quickly move on to the next one.
- Let go of yesterday's successes and focus on being successful today so that you will be unstoppable tomorrow.
- Each success is a building block toward a larger future goal.

Remember these principles, especially if you are an employee. Put together the recommendations in this book to help you reach your potential, and with your newfound knowledge, you'll quickly be on your way to moving up the ladder. Once again, this is no one else's responsibility but yours, because…

If You Don't Care, Who Will?

No one else will ever care as much about your success as you!

You need to start caring about yourself. Again, as long as your purpose for doing so is "others focused," there is nothing wrong with taking care of yourself. Every time I get on an airplane, I am reminded of the importance of taking care of myself, so that I, in turn, can take care of others. On virtually every flight I've ever taken, an attendant has given the same instructions before taking off. It goes something like this: "In the event of an emergency, the oxygen masks will drop from the compartments above. Please make sure that you place the mask securely on *yourself* before helping any other passengers with their masks." This is a great reminder that you need to take care of yourself, or you will not be any help to others. Being motivated for life means that you must maximize your own potential and take care of yourself first, in order to help more people in more ways.

As I write this, I am on a six-week break from work due to a fall in which I broke my right foot. I can't place any weight on it, because the pins that were inserted to help the bones heal properly might break, which would necessitate another surgery. Being unable to walk for the next few weeks has given me time to focus on other aspects of my motivated life. At the same time, my business needs to keep moving forward even in my absence. I'm reminded of the importance of taking care of myself. While I have plenty of help from others, and I haven't been shy at all about asking for help, no one is going to take care of all of the different aspects of my life for me. If I'm not taking care of my business, whether I am physically present or not, it will not run the same way (even with the proper procedures in place). Part of my energy still needs to go toward its success. If I don't take care of my health, no one else is going to track me down and force me to get well and stay healthy. If I don't take the time right now to sit down and write this book, no one else is going to do it for me. If I'm not focused and motivated to create the life that I want for myself, I can assure you that no one else is going to make it perfect for me. And only when I take care of myself will I then be able to help others to maximize their lives.

When it comes right down to it, most of your accomplishments really are only valued by you. I remember learning this lesson in high school sports. After my freshman season in wrestling, in which I fell short of my goal of becoming a state champion, my sophomore season was filled with greater success. I put in more effort and energy following my freshman loss in the state finals to ensure victory the following year. I had built up the rewards of becoming a state champion so much in my mind that I was willing to do almost anything to win. My sophomore season, I achieved my goal of becoming a state champion in my weight class.

As I was walking off of the center-stage wrestling mat at the arena, I shook hands with my coaches, hugged my father who was nearby, and then he and I walked quietly into the hallway, where we smiled together by ourselves. To this day, I am not quite sure what I expected, but I'd certainly expected more than this. No students rushing the arena to congratulate me, no chants of my name, no songs on the loudspeakers in my honor. The announcer simply called out the names of the next competitors, and competition resumed. My coaches and teammates were proud and my family and friends were happy for my success, but when it came right down to it, I cared more than anyone else really did. Had I lost, my coaches and teammates would have *still* been there for me and my family would have *still* loved me and been happy I'd made it that far.

It was then that I realized that, after setting my goal, working excessively to achieve it, and finally making it a reality, I was the only one who *really* cared. Everyone else was really focused on themselves and their own lives throughout the time that I'd put in all of the extra effort to achieve my goals—as they should have been. Let's face it, not everyone achieves a goal and has a day named in their honor for it. Not everyone gets a homecoming parade to celebrate their accomplishments. You're the only one who will care about most of your goals and accomplishments. Only you will receive the true feeling of success in those accomplishments. However, as I've learned through this process, I can create more leverage by building up the ending in my mind, even when I know that the fireworks surrounding the result will only occur inside of my head. Even now, I've continued to build goals up in my mind to give me the necessary drive and leverage to stay motivated.

You need to take care of you. Design the life that you want. Remember that no one else is going to do it for you. Your boss is not going to go out of his or her way to make sure that your bank account is healthy. Your boss's job is to pay you a fair wage for the work you provide. It's your job to make sure that you *do* the right things with your money once paid. The same applies for employers. Your employees are there to provide the work required for a fee. No one is going to go above and beyond unless you expect them to and hold them accountable. It is your business, not theirs. So be mindful of the fact that your success, while possibly also dependent upon the work of your employees, is still your responsibility.

In fact, this principal applies to every aspect of your life. Make the connection and starting doing the things necessary to take care of you. Take care of *your* health, *your* family, *your* church, *your* work, *your* finances… and everything else in *your* life. It is the only way that you will ever truly achieve a motivated life, and only then will you be able to best serve others.

Success Strategies

- Start caring more about your own success.
- If you don't take care of yourself, you won't be much good to anyone else.
- Only you will receive the true feeling of success when accomplishing your goals.
- Design the life that you want and remember that no one else is going to do it for you.
- Success in helping others must first occur by helping yourself.

Chapter 4

PERSONAL RESPONSIBILITY

Once you've sincerely learned that you are worth the effort and that you have everything that you need right now to start living a motivated life, you'll need to start betting on yourself. In John Maxwell's book *The Difference Maker*, he writes about becoming the person who can make a positive difference in any situation. You will need to see yourself as a person who brings to the table something special in every aspect of life.

Learn to Bet on Yourself

Whether your goal requires your personal effort or those of a team, you'll only accomplish your potential when you see yourself as a "difference maker." Successful people who live a motivated life believe that the missing ingredient to any challenge is themselves. They always look inward for solutions and bet on their own abilities for future success.

I'm always intrigued by the excuses that people will throw out for their shortcomings, especially in team settings. Most of the time, people are quick to blame someone or something other than themselves. They'll speak as though their challenges were outside of their control. They see themselves as having no ownership in their success or failure, but rather see only other people's efforts (or lack thereof) as the cause of their

challenges or failures. These unsuccessful and unmotivated people use
excuses like

- "He didn't do…"
- "She didn't do…"
- "It was too early."
- "It was too late."
- "There wasn't enough time."
- "They didn't prepare properly."
- "We weren't given enough training."
- "The weather wasn't right."
- "It was too hot."
- "It was too cold."
- "Monday was the wrong day."
- "Friday was the wrong day."

And the list goes on and on. As you will see, not one of these excuses
contains the word "I." However, in any challenge, that is the only thing
that you can truly control. In contrast with these answers, the people who
are living a motivated life give responses like

- "Next time I'll work harder"
- "I didn't prepare enough, but I'll know how to do things better
  next time"
- "I could have done…"
- "Next time I will…"

Get the idea? You're the only variable over which you have any
control. You alone have the ability to change your circumstances. You
alone can choose to be a "difference maker" in your life and the lives of
others. Your thoughts and your actions are the only things that you can
truly control. So if you are not already doing so, take control today. Begin

seeing yourself as the answer to all of the challenges that life presents; as the one person who can make a difference. Once you begin to see yourself in this light, you'll find that most of the challenges that you're currently facing will start to resolve. Even more importantly, you'll be willing to accept greater challenges due to your confidence in your own abilities.

I have found that it's easiest to think this way when completing tasks for which you're solely responsible, but as I just told you; this is *still* possible to do in-group settings.

Let me give you an example. After successfully opening and sustaining a business in which I worked and in which I was present on a daily basis, I decided to open a second location. This new location would be modeled exactly on my already-successful business, but would be run by others, not myself. This idea worked out great in the beginning, and I saw myself as able to accomplish anything I set my mind to. However, after a few months went by, things were not going as I'd hoped. At that point, I could have easily blamed the workers in the second office for the lack of success. In fact, I truly believe, and have heard, that most other people in similar circumstances react this way. But instead of succumbing to those tempting thoughts, I looked inward for both the ownership of the challenges as well as the potential solutions. I realized that, in both offices, I was still able to bet on myself and my capabilities; it would just require different personal strengths to accomplish success in each of the businesses. I thought:

- "I can't blame the people, because *I* hired them."
- "They are not doing things properly yet, because *I* haven't thoroughly trained them."
- "They're not achieving their goals, because *I* have not held them accountable."
- "*My* leadership needs to improve if the office is going to be successful."

Do you see the difference? Stop blaming others for what's going in your life. You can only control yourself, and within yourself lies every answer to every problem that you will ever face. See yourself as the solution, and then do the things necessary to achieve the result that you want.

Do you recall the famous words of John F. Kennedy? "Ask not what your country can do for you, but what you can do for your country." Since all solutions come from within, you can say the same for any other area of your life:

- Ask not what my team can do for me, but what I can do for my team.

- Ask not what my teachers can do for me, but what I can do for my teachers.

- Ask not what my staff can do for me, but what I can do for my staff.

- Ask not what my friends can do for me, but what I can do for my friends.

- Ask not what my family can do for me, but what I can do for my family.

- Ask not what my church can do for me, but what I can do for my church.

- Ask not what my spouse can do for me, but what I can do for my spouse.

Notice the two key words in JFK's speech, as well as in my examples: "I" and "do." You are responsible, and what you *do* will lead you to your potential.

Start seeing everything in your life from this perspective right now. Once you begin, you'll see greater possibilities. And once you've been successful in the little things, you'll begin to place more responsibility on yourself for the big things that life has in store for you. You'll begin to bet on yourself! As in the previous business example, I continually look for ways in which to challenge myself to do better today than I did yesterday.

And I plan to put even more responsibility on myself tomorrow. If your current goals revolve solely around your own physical presence, then see yourself as physically able to handle any situation. And if your goals revolve around others' actions, as in a coaching situation or a business situation, begin to see your knowledge, your leadership, and your attitude as the difference in your future success. When you do, you'll find yourself gaining momentum toward a crucial element of your success, that of....

Energy

The fun part about being motivated for life is that you'll begin to take action toward achieving the life that you want, and you will get more energy from the actions that you take. Have you ever run into one of those days when you're surprised by one disaster after another? I'll bet that you have. And how did you feel by the end of the day? Exhausted! When you're reacting to events rather than taking *proactive* action, you become drained of your energy. Now, while reacting to unexpected events is occasionally unavoidable, I've found that too many people simply react to life on a daily basis rather than taking active control of their lives. Filling your days with reactions, rather than *actions*, will never lead you to a truly motivated life.

In contrast, have you ever begun a new exercise program after a period of inactivity? If so, what happens? After the initial few days of learning the new routine, you begin to feel more energized. Here you are, losing calories and burning energy, yet by taking action, you're giving yourself *more* energy as a result!

I've even found this to be true in competitive sports as well. The person who takes the offensive, creates the action, and acts first, actually uses *less* energy than the person reacting to their actions—even though they may be doing more physically!

Action creates energy, and reaction creates fatigue.

This is important, because if there's any *one* thing that you need to achieve the motivated life you hope for, it's energy.

- Want to improve as an athlete?
- Want to improve as a coach?
- Want to improve as a mother or father?
- Want to have a better marriage?
- Want to be a better friend?
- Want to have a more fulfilling job?
- Want to have a better physique?

If so, apply more energy today! You'll be on your way to more of everything immediately.

Success Strategies

- Look inward for solutions and learn to bet on your own abilities.
- You are the only person whom you can control.
- You alone have the ability to change your current circumstances.
- Within yourself lies every answer to every problem that you will ever face.
- Action creates energy and reaction creates fatigue.

In sum, a truly motivated life will require more energy. And with more energy, you will no longer have any fear of....

Taking Risks

> *Progress always involves risk. You can't steal second base and keep your foot on first.* —Frederick B. Wilcox

Every successful person has taken a risk. Without exception, you cannot become successful in any endeavor if you never step out of your comfort zone and take a chance. For my part, most of the times I succeed,

I first put myself in a position to *fail*…then worked through the process to find a way to succeed. The question that has been posed to me, and that I now give to you is what would you do if success were guaranteed? Think about the answer right now. If failure were not an option, what would you do differently? If your answer to this question is anything different than what you are currently doing, then you need to start thinking more positively. The realist in all of us obviously knows that success in never truly guaranteed, but you must also realize that you are capable of *anything* if you decide that you want it badly enough.

As God's chosen sons and daughters, we are expected to
attempt something large enough that failure is guaranteed…
unless God steps in. —Dr. Bruce Wilkinson

Jordan declared at the end of the commercial, "Because I have failed, I succeed." We all remember Michael Jordan as one of the greatest basketball players of all times, yet think of the risk that he took each time the ball was in his hands in the final seconds of a close game. Sometimes it worked out well for him, and sometimes it didn't. Regardless, he was willing to accept the risk. Motivated people want control of their own destinies.

When I opened my first business shortly after graduating from chiropractic school, I also took on a major risk. In order to start the business, I took out $110,000 home equity loan against my parents' house. Do you think I was motivated to be successful, knowing that my parents could lose their house if I failed? You'd better believe I was! However, I was willing to accept the risk because I knew that my effort and my motivation would determine my success. If the fate of their home was in someone else's hands, or if the success of my business was in someone else's hands, I wouldn't have taken the same risk. I accepted the risk because it was all on me. And because I took on a much greater risk, I received a much greater reward in the end.

The important thing to learn here is that the bigger the risk, the bigger the reward. If you risk little, you only stand to gain little. We all wish that we could play like Michael Jordan on the basketball court, but how many of us would willingly accept the risks involved in taking the final shot in the final seconds of the game, with an arena filled with screaming fans and a television audience of millions? Unmotivated people want the reward without any risk. In contrast, to the Michael Jordans of the world, the risk of allowing the game-winning shot to rest in someone else's hands is intolerable.

Whether you're looking for a motivated life in sports, in business, in relationships, or in life, you must accept risk as a necessary part of your success. But let me point out to you that risk taking is by no means foreign to you. You take on more risks each day than you are aware of. It is all of matter of your perspective. To employers, being an employee looks risky, because you have limited control of your future. To employees, being an employer looks risky because much of the potential success rests on your own shoulders. Even when it comes to driving a car, there's tremendous risk involved. If you get in a car as a driver, your life and the lives of everyone else in your car now rests with you. As a passenger, your life is now in the hands of the driver of the vehicle. These are some of the most extreme risks that we could possibly take; yet we pay them no attention and make potentially life-altering decisions passively each day. The risks that I'm suggesting are nowhere close to the risk that you already accept each day in these situations. But what I'm suggesting is that you take *intentional* risks. More importantly, take intentional risks that are dependent on *your* ability and *your* determination. As you've learned in the previous chapter, the most effective and potentially life-changing risk that you can take is to bet on yourself.

With this in mind, look back to the question that I posed to you. What would you do if success were guaranteed? Dream bigger. Accept the risk. Remember, in most aspects of your life, the risk that you accept will be much less than the risk you take simply getting in your car each day. Don't be afraid to jump in the deep end of the pool. All of the successful people ahead of you have had to do it themselves at some point. Once you're in the water, your newfound motivation will force you to swim. If you're determined to make it to your destination no matter what happens, then risk doesn't feel like risk at all.

Success Strategies

- Every successful person has taken a risk. The greater the risk, the greater the reward.

- What would you do if success were guaranteed?

- Your own effort and your own motivation will determine your level of success.

- Unmotivated people want the reward without having to risk anything.

- If you are determined to succeed, then risk doesn't feel like risk at all.

These principles are especially true when your goal is to create the....

Chapter 5

STEPPING STONES

One of your new goals should be to aim so high in all that you do, that you also inspire others to be their best. Too many times in life, we set meager goals that not only do not excite us, but also do not inspire others. The goals that we are striving for, the missions that we have in life, should challenge us to be more than we ever hoped to be. However, they should also inspire others to dream bigger.

Inspire Others

In dealing with numerous people over the years, it has been my observation that virtually no one actually considers themselves leaders. However, when looking at these same people from the outside, *I* consider them leaders. Right now, I want you to think of someone close to you whom you admire. Ten bucks says that they don't know how you feel that about them, and that they don't consider themselves to be a leader. If they knew that you were watching them as closely as you probably are, they'd probably be less likely to allow you to be persuaded by their decisions, for fear that they might steer you in the wrong direction by accident. However, whether you see yourself as a leader or not, there's at least one person—and often many people—who are watching what you do. Still don't believe me? Here's a really simple example for you to test this theory. (If you've ever played a round of golf with someone, this example will bring you straight to the point. If not, I guarantee that anyone who's played golf will affirm to you that this example rings true.)

When I first began playing golf several years ago, I went out with friends to have some fun and learn the game. We never took ourselves too seriously, especially me, since my friends had already been playing for quite a while when I first began. Inevitably, my friends would ask me at the end of each hole what I had scored. Since I was so bad that I obviously wasn't about to win any awards and wasn't in danger of being the low scorer for the day, I would quickly add up my score and report it to them. As is human nature, I would forget a stroke at least once every time we went to play. I wasn't intentionally leaving out this extra stroke, but was merely so focused on correcting my swing that I calculated incorrectly. Without exception, if I reported one less stroke than I had actually swung, my friends would point out and correct my error. Often, they would not only point out each stroke that I'd made, but the exact position of my ball location, my club selection, and even the poor results of each hit. After a while, I learned that this was the case regardless of who was in my group.

The result of this experience is that I'm now extremely precise with my number of swings. I now know that, just because I'm not in the hunt to win the game, that doesn't stop everyone from watching my every move and keeping tabs on my game and the decisions that I make.

This is often the case with life. We arbitrarily go through our day making decisions that seem to be minuscule, and we think that these decisions will affect no one but ourselves. I'm telling you that every decision you make will affect someone, be it positively or negatively. If now is the first time you've realized that you're always leading someone else, let this be motivation to make better decisions and direct your future so you inspire others. You do not have to be the top of your organization, the team captain, or the boss to make decisions and set goals that will inspire other people. You also do not have to be that person who's constantly telling other people what they should do, or how you would have done something differently. As my wrestling coach and mentor, Reverend Nate

Carr, always used to say, "Let what you do speak so loudly that people can't hear what you say."

I'm saying not only to let your actions speak for themselves, but to make sure that those actions are inspiring to both yourself and others.

If you're still looking for additional motivation, think about this: how will your decisions potentially inspire your children (or the children you plan to have)? Are you settling for less than you would urge them to go for? If the answer is yes, you need to read the quote in the last paragraph again! Kids are not nearly as interested in what you say as what you do. If you're trying to teach your kids that anything is possible for them, then you need to start believing it yourself right now, to the point that you act upon it immediately. Trust me, you won't need to tell everyone that you're changing your own standards and expectations; they'll notice. And if you happen to be reading this and already have grown children, remember that you can never be too old to be an inspiration. Become an inspiration today!

Success Strategies

- Choose goals that will inspire others to be their best also.
- Make wise choices in both the large and small matters of your life.
- Even small decisions have potentially large effects on yourself and others.
- Every decision you make will affect someone.
- People follow what you do more than what you say.

In order to aim higher than you have ever aimed in your entire life, you'll have to start...

Setting Your Goals

I have absolutely no limitations to
what I plan to create. —Napoleon Hill

To me, this is the most fun part of the process of becoming motivated for life. I love to dream big. And every time I do, I recall Walt Disney. If he could dream up a place as spectacular as Disney World, why can't I dream of doing something equally great in my lifetime? Why can't you dream of being everything that you were meant to be in your lifetime? As you start to imagine what you're possible of achieving, don't let your mind revert back to "realistic" thinking. Realistic is boring. Realistic is uninspired. Realistic is not motivational! Remember that, when you limit yourself to "realistic," someone else in the world will actually accomplish the dreams you could have reached if you'd thought bigger and taken action.

> *Unhappiness is...not knowing what we want and*
> *killing ourselves to get it.* —Don Herald

If you have never dreamed big before, this is a huge step toward creating the life that you want. If these goals are never defined, then you will never be working toward anything. I'm constantly amazed at the number of people I talk to that are unhappy with their lives, yet who have no idea what would make them happy. When you define what it is that you want, you'll find that the world has a way of working things out for you. To reverse the quote above, you could say that happiness is knowing what you want and knowing that you'll get it!

So let's establish some dreams right now. In the following section, I want you to list three things in each category. Be sure to file this form in your Motivational Binder. The categories are *be*, *do*, and *have*. Don't feel limited by this form. If you have fifteen different things to add to each of these categories, then do it. Three items in each category is only a starting point. Also, we will come back to these goals in a few chapters and add timelines to them. For now, I want you to dream big and get it done!

> *Unless you attempt more than you can possibly do,*
> *you'll never achieve all that you can do.* —John Maxwell

List three things you want to be:

1. _____

2. _____

3. _____

List three things you want to do:

1. _____

2. _____

3. _____

List three things you want to have:

1. _____

2. _____

3. _____

Once you have established your purpose, you must establish where you are. And once you know where you are, you will be able to start to plan specific *be*, *do*, and *have* goals for your future. Skipping this step would be the equivalent of saying, "I want to lose ten pounds" and not knowing how much you weigh right now. You'd know where you are going, but you wouldn't know where you were starting. So, to determine where you are right now, simply revisit your answers to the previous *be, do,* and *have* questions. Are you currently acting like the person you want to be? Are you moving in that direction? Are you currently doing the things you want to do? Are you moving in that direction? Do you currently have the things you want to have? Are you moving in that direction? If your answer to these questions is no, don't worry, you are not alone. However, we will change that by the time you're done reading this book.

Now look at your personal Purpose Statement. Are you currently working to live out your mission? If not, this is the place to start your journey toward your own unique, motivated life. Your purpose doesn't care where you start. You can begin to live your mission today—right this second. By beginning to live out your purpose, you will immediately put yourself on the path to a motivated life.

To make this more concrete, let's use my own purpose as an example. My mission is "to lead others to health, wealth, and better lives." Let's say that you have a similar mission, but in your life, you're currently dissatisfied with your work and feel as though your effort does not make a difference. I'll bet you could find a way to do a better job of achieving your purpose today. You shouldn't think so much about your lousy clients, your incompetent coworkers, your miserable staff, or your jerk of a boss. Your mission is to *help* those other people rather than yourself. The irony lies in the fact that the only way to maximize your ability to help others is to motivate *yourself* to do so.

Definiteness of purpose is the starting point of all achievement and its lack is the stumbling block. —W. Clement Stone

Success Strategies

- Dream big. Realistic goals are boring.
- Happiness is knowing what you want and knowing that you will get it.
- What are your top three *be, do, have* desires?
- You can begin to work toward your goals today.
- The bigger your goals, the more people you can help.

Now that you've planned out exactly what you want, let's make each of these goals amazingly easy to attain by....

Breaking it Down

Once you have determined exactly what it is that you want, it's time to take each aspect of your motivated life one step further. You will now need to break down each area of life that you wish to improve into smaller pieces. By doing this, you will see how easy it really is to make simple changes to what you think and what you do to accomplish amazing results.

In an interview, Billy Joel defined himself as "competent." Keep in mind he's an acclaimed musician and one of the most successful recording artists of all times! He went on to explain that, in order to be extraordinary as an artist, he needed to break down the different aspects involved in reaching his potential and learn to be good at each individual facet. He explained that he needed to know how to write, how to sing, how to play, and how to perform. He denied any specific genius involved in his achievements and attributed all of his success to his competence in each of these areas.

So let's take a few minutes now to determine exactly what skills and strengths you'll need to reach each specific goal. Simply write the various aspects involved in achieving each goal in subcategories beneath the actual goal itself. Remember to include this breakdown in your Motivational Binder. Here's an example of possible subcategories for mini-goals:

Goal: To be the best athlete that I can be

Subcategories for Mini-Goals:

- Technique
- Strength
- Conditioning
- Coaching
- Competition

Goal: To be the best physician that I can be

Subcategories for Mini-Goals:

- Ability to diagnose
- Ability to treat
- People skills

- Ability to educate
- Ability to market
- Ability to manage staff

You'll find yourself accomplishing your dreams much more easily once you have broken down the big goal into these smaller pieces, allowing you to conquer each of these smaller aspects in a shorter amount of time and with less effort than it will take to accomplish the larger dream. You'll gain energy and confidence as you begin to check these mini-goals off your list en route to completing the larger picture.

You don't have to stop at the sort of categories I've listed in the example above; mini-goals can always be broken down into even smaller pieces if you are so inclined. Obviously, the smaller the piece, the easier it will be to accomplish. Instead of looking for a home run or a quick fix to accomplish your goals, begin thinking about achieving your potential with a series of base hits. Being good at each small piece of the puzzle will culminate in a great result. And by breaking down your goals into smaller pieces, you'll avoid being overwhelmed by the size of your dreams.

As an example, if you'd like to lose twenty pounds, you are much more likely to accomplish this goal if you focus on losing two pounds per week. Those who continue to look solely at the broader picture will be easily discouraged if the process seems to be taking too long or if they fall short of their goal. Twenty pounds begins to seem like a huge amount, and one that they really don't feel like working toward. However, if you're focusing on the smaller victories, losing two pounds per week is something that seems much more easily attainable. And in addition to that, every time you experience success, your drive to complete the larger goal increases, as it appears much more attainable.

To give a personal example of how I met a business goal, I have been a client of a group called Integrity Management for several years. Integrity Management advises physicians about how to grow their practices. Keith Maule, now CEO and chief motivator for the company, has implemented a "five-year plan" strategy into all of his clients' coaching calls. New Integrity clients start out with their own ideas of what their ultimate practice will look like, based on their individual philosophies, techniques, capacities, and goals. Some see themselves as solo practitioners in a six-day-per-week job. Others envision running multiple doctors' offices or multiple clinics in which they become the "clinic director" and only treat patients themselves on an as-needed basis.

There is really no right or wrong answer to what the clients desire, but answering their questions served as a great benchmark for where the coaches were trying to get us. For my part, when I first looked at the number of new chiropractic patients that I wanted to acquire each month and the number of times I believed each patient should receive a chiropractic adjustment, I was overwhelmed. Integrity Management had made a list of my company's current office statistics, including how many new patients we acquired each month, how many times the average patient returned, and what our collection amount was on each visit. Based on where our numbers were currently at, it seemed impossible. Yet with Integrity Management's five-year plan in place, we worked backward one year at a time in each of the three categories, and established a plan for how to reach our goals based on one-year increments. Suddenly, we had taken the larger goal, broken it into smaller pieces, and then came up with a plan to help more people in slightly larger amounts each year. Not only did this allow us to reach all of our goals, but we have been able to help significantly more people gain and maintain optimum health through chiropractic care, simply because we broke our goals into smaller pieces and began accomplishing the mini-successes that would eventually lead to the business of my dreams.

Success Strategies

- To achieve success, begin with the larger goals and work backward.
- Divide each larger goal into smaller pieces and achieve one piece at a time.

- Conquering smaller goals gives you energy and confidence as you approach the large goal.

- Smaller goals keep you from being overwhelmed by the bigger picture.

- Even small goals can always be divided into smaller pieces.

When you apply this principle to your own life, you will learn that you, and you alone, are....

Chapter 6

YOUR ONLY COMPETITION

As the popular saying goes, "Amateurs compete with others. Professionals compete with themselves." Indeed, truly motivated people in any field will always have a few things in common:

- The relentless pursuit of their purpose.

- The relentless pursuit of their goals.

- The relentless pursuit of unattainable perfection in everything they do.

Once you have defined a purpose outside of yourself, along with specific *be*, *do*, and *have* goals, you will then be motivated to achieve perfection in all that you do. Perfection is unattainable, but the pursuit of perfection is eternal for the motivated life. You are always looking at ways to get better and do better in every aspect of your life. The key in doing so is to concentrate on changing and perfecting the only thing over which you truly have any control: you.

By living a motivated life with a purpose outside of yourself, your only competition becomes *you*. You are no longer focused on bringing others down so that you can feel more important. You are no longer worried about what everyone else is doing. Your goal is to be motivated to achieve your own purpose. And if your purpose is one that you have defined to be *selfless* rather than selfish, accomplishing your goals will help others as well.

Even in competitive sports, where you may be competing one-on-one with your competition, you can only be responsible for what you do. Either you are acting first, causing your opponent to react, or your opponent is acting first, causing you to *react*. Either way, you can't control your opposition's choices; you can only control yourself.

In team sports, you'll find that the most successful athletes always take responsibility for their teams. They are quick to say "I" when things don't go their way, and quick to say "we" when they do. Even if it would be easy to blame the defense for a loss, you'll never hear superstar quarterback Peyton Manning speak about anyone else's ownership but his own. Rather than pointing fingers at others, he always finds the incomplete plays that he was responsible for, and takes ownership for the outcome himself. He then works relentlessly to make sure that his next game is better and that he has corrected his mistakes from the previous game. Because he takes responsibility for the team, he is great. Motivated athletes take personal ownership of what needs to be improved. They want control of the game in the final seconds. And, when things do not work out in their favor, they still take full responsibility. These people serve as great, motivational inspirations to everyone because they compete against themselves and work to control the only person that they can truly change: themselves.

Healthy Competition

Let me interject that I love competition. I believe that instituting healthy competition into your daily life will help you to stay motivated. As a competitive person, I continually look for ways to incorporate competition with others into my day. Many times, this competition is not officially announced; it just takes place in my mind. But once again, the competition is created with the hopes of driving me to *my* potential. When viewed in the proper light, competition is essential in getting the most out of yourself. Virtually every successful athlete I know is driven to do the extra work necessary to be their best, even when no one else is watching. They will put in the extra time that it takes to push themselves to the utmost, both mentally and physically. Yet, if you were to take any single athlete, regardless of their sport, and ask them run a 200-meter sprint by themselves, their results would not be as good as if they were running next to someone trying to beat them. That extra competition will help to push them to *be, do,* and *have* more. Physically, how does a person running next to them really affect them? Not at all. But mentally, that extra incentive is everything.

I believe that the same holds true in business. Whether you are in a truly competitive business or not, I believe that placing yourself in some sort of competition will force you to concentrate on being your best. Whether you are competing with your coworkers, your staff, your boss, or with another business, the key to healthy competition is remembering that it is essentially *you* against *you.* By remembering who your true competition is at all times, you'll avoid the daily excuses that inevitably creep in when you compete with other people, rather than with yourself:

- "They're not working as hard as I am."
- "They're cheating."
- "They, they, they!"

Stop worrying about *them* and concentrate on *you.* Control your effort. Control your thoughts. Keep your mind on your business. Control what you do!

In staff meetings to assess our business goals, I've found that motivated employees will always talk about what they can do personally to bring us closer to achieving our mission. The unmotivated employees will throw out ideas for others to do, but want no part in the action needed to reach our purpose. They typically throw out ideas that start with the word "someone," as in, "Someone needs to…" Those who say "I will…" always end up with longer tenures and better rewards than unmotivated employees who are not self-driven to take personal responsibility to be their best, and in turn, to benefit the team. If you are an employer, begin immediately to recognize those who are motivated and start rewarding their actions. If you are an employee, begin to take responsibility today, and do what you know you *can* and *should* do to be your best. Nothing bad can possibly come from being your best. If you are not recognized for it, your skills and motivation will still serve you well in future endeavors.

I cannot stress to you the importance of *doing*. The world responds to and rewards action. Take action yourself, and take action today. Your only competition is you. Stop worrying about what everyone else is or isn't doing, and think about the things that require action today. Follow Nike's advice; "Just do it!"

The biggest problem with competing against others rather than yourself is that you will begin making unhealthy comparisons. Use others to drive you to be your best, but don't make comparisons that will bring you down. There is only one you. And whether you are the best or not is not nearly as important as whether you are *your* best.

One of my favorite athletes named Ray displayed this attribute as well as anyone I know. Ray was an extraordinary wrestler when he was younger, and entered college as the number-one recruit in the country. In addition to being a wrestler, Ray is a very intelligent individual with some very interesting idiosyncrasies. As a hobby, Ray also plays chess, and after he was recruited to wrestle for Iowa University, he also became a member of the university's chess team. Much like Josh Waitzkin, whom you will learn about in a later chapter, Ray used his intelligence and problem-solving ability to excel in the sport of wrestling, and then translated those same abilities into success in the game of chess.

Ray had a very successful wrestling career in college, but never rose to the full expectations of his coaches or the fans of Iowa University. I read an interview of Ray as he was getting ready to graduate, in which he was asked about his failure to meet other people's expectations in wrestling. He was asked if his preoccupation with chess was a possible distraction. Ray responded by saying, "I'm the best chess player on the wrestling team, and by far the best wrestler on the chess team." Instead of going with the interviewer's direction of pointing out his inadequacies, he was focused on those aspects of himself that made him unique and extraordinary in his own right—and that made him his best in all areas of life.

Success Strategies

- Perfection is unattainable, but its pursuit is endless for successful people.

- Successful team members say "I" when things don't go their way, and "we" when they do.

- Successful people want the ball in their hands when the game is on the line.

- All competition is essentially you against you. Focus on being *your* best rather than *the* best.

- Surround yourself with people who will push you to be your best.

- Stop focusing on your inabilities and start concentrating on your abilities.

- Stop comparing yourself to others and start competing with yourself to be the best you can be.

Competing with yourself becomes must simpler when you follow the....

Four Keys to Unstoppable Success

Tiger Woods *is* Tiger Woods *because he never hits the snooze button*
—Bill Stewart, head football coach for West Virginia University

Before I opened my first business, I listened to an audio series that gave me some of the best advice I could have ever received. Not only did the advice apply to successfully running a business, it also applied to virtually every aspect of leading a motivated life. I have continually used this advice to hold myself accountable in sports, in business, and in life. As a coach, I have found that the most successful athletes follow these rules. As an employer, I have found that I have promoted those who have followed these rules. I have also found that, without exception, every employee that has been terminated was unable to follow one or more of these rules. Learn these rules and implement them into your life to help you achieve your goals:

- Always show up on time.

The best of the best always show up! This rule is all about keeping and honoring your commitments. You must understand that in order to live a motivated life, you have to value the importance of *today*. And once you understand the importance of today, you will learn the importance of making each minute count during today. That means showing up on time and using that time in the most productive way possible. The difference between motivated people and everyone else is that they show up on time because it is the right thing to do—not just because someone else wants them to. If you've ever seen a list of Tiger Woods's daily training agenda, you will understand why he is the best. You must also realize that Tiger Woods doesn't *have* to do anything. No one is forcing him to be the best. Chances are that, by this point, he could practice very little and still do very well in competitions. However, he cannot be his best unless he forces himself to show up on time and honor the commitment to excellence that he has made to himself.

Likewise, Donald Trump doesn't *need* to work. Just like Tiger, he could retire today and continue to maintain a very wealthy lifestyle from his current businesses and assets. But it is his drive to be his best that gets him to expand his empire on a daily basis. Every day that he's alive, he is working to increase his wealth. While he has a tremendous amount of assistance from his business managers and advisers, he is still motivated to show up on time and honor his commitments. If you've ever seen an episode of *The Apprentice*, you'll remember the importance that each of the team's advisers placed on timeliness for the project managers. Not only does Donald Trump show up on time to honor his commitments, but he expected nothing less from his current and potential employees.

If you are not currently showing up for your commitments on time, make the decision to change today. You will be amazed at how much more you will accomplish with each day. You will also find that others will find comfort in your newfound reliability.

- Always say "please" and "thank you."

There's no such thing as a self-made man. I've had much help and have found that if you are willing to work, many people are willing to help you. —O. Wayne Rollins

There are two major parts to this key: "please" *and* "thank you." One without the other will not work. In order to live a motivated life, you need to implement *both* of them.

The first, "please," involves asking for help. Think about it. This word really only comes into play when you are asking someone else to help you to achieve a goal. If you are going to achieve the life of your dreams, you have to be willing to continually ask for help. "Please" is a simple word that, when used, will help to attract others to your cause.

"Please" is also a word of positive attitude. Anytime you ask for help and use the word "please," people also get the feeling that you'll be thankful for their help. Especially in business, I have found that this is one of the most underutilized words of necessity. When dealing with coworkers and with customers, clients, or patients, simply using the word "please" will avoid more controversy than anything else.

A motivated life will require not only a positive attitude, but also help from others, so start making this word a staple in your vocabulary today.

The words "thank you" also involve having a positive attitude. What I've noticed about simply using the words "thank you" is that they not only put a final stamp on the help that you have just received, but also automatically increase your chances of receiving additional help in the future. If people know that you appreciate their help, they'll be more apt to give you assistance again. Leaving the words out and assuming that people know you're thankful is a major miscalculation. Actually, the opposite is true—people assume that you *did not* and *do not* appreciate their help unless you say it.

If you really want to have fun, say "thank you" to people who don't expect it. You'll be amazed at how far this simple gesture will go. For example, while I was in school, I was fortunate enough to get a part-time job in a chiropractic office. Even though I was a poor, broke college student, I was not working for the money, but rather for the experience. After the first two weeks, I had already learned more about running a business than I had learned in the previous three years of school. At the same time, I was actually being paid for my time to be there. When my first paycheck came, I began to put myself in the clinic director's place. Here he was, teaching me how to run my own facility one day, and at the same time, paying me to be there. Even though I was not interested in volunteering, since I really *did* need the money, it still seemed as if he was giving more to me than I was to him. I called him after that first paycheck arrived and told him that I simply wanted to thank him. I told him that I was appreciative of the opportunity to learn from him, and that it didn't seem fair that I was also being paid. To my surprise, he was dumbfounded. He said, "Are you actually just calling to say thanks?"

I replied, "Yes. That's all." He told me that in four years of practice, this was the first time that a staff member had ever said "thank you" for anything. As a staff member, I knew that other staff members were thankful as well, but none of them had ever actually told him. Not only was I already getting more from him than I was able to give at the time, but after he knew how thankful I was, he began to put even more effort into helping me with anything and everything that I needed. All because I said "thank you"!

A short time later, running my own clinics, I began to understand how he must have felt. As an employer, I was working as hard as possible to make sure that all of our staff members remained employed and were paid appropriately for their work, yet I never received a thank you. Having been on the other side of the equation, I knew that *not* hearing the words didn't mean that everyone was automatically ungrateful, yet hearing the words would have been a nice touch in return for my efforts. Whether you're a child with a parent to thank, a student with a teacher to thank, an athlete with a coach to thank, a husband or wife with a spouse to thank, an employee with an employer to thank, or an employer with employees to thank, I encourage you to go out of your way to tell them "thank you" today and every day.

The importance of having an "attitude of gratitude" can never be overstated. Living a motivated life means that you not only hold yourself to a higher level of expectations and accountability, but also that you are thankful every step of the way. Again, since you will need help achieving and maintaining a motivated life, you need to incorporate both "please" and "thank you" into every phase of your existence. You will not only avoid undue criticism for being ungrateful for the help of others, but you will also encourage others to actually *want* to help you.

- Always do what you say you will do

In my opinion, this is where the biggest gap exists in reaching you own potential. This gap lies between talking and doing. Countless dreams have never and will never come true due to this gap between what people say and what they actually *do*. Unfortunately, for most people, this gap means they'll never achieve their dreams.

Once you have dreamed of what you want in your life, I believe wholeheartedly in the importance of speaking your dream. Saying what you want to accomplish over and over and over will increase your chances of achieving it astronomically. However, just as important as what you dream and what you say is what you *do*. The most successful people the world has ever known have accomplished great things, not only because they dream a bigger dream than others, but because they have *done* exactly what it takes to make the dream come true.

How many times have you been let down by a politician who, after making one promise after another to improve everyone's lives (including yours), failed to do a single thing they said once elected? How many times have you been let down by coworkers who said they'd do one thing or another, only to leave you short of your goal, or equally annoyingly, leaving you to do their work?

I have countless memories of teammates speaking boldly at the onset of a new year about what they were going to *do* this year:

- "This year we're going to out-work everyone in the world!"
- "This year we're going to be the best ever!"
- "This year we're going to…!"

But once the time to make these things happen finally arrived, they were nowhere to be found. Their talk was huge, but their actions were not there to back them up.

On the other hand, think of the times when people have spoken about their future and then have *done* exactly what they said they would do. I'll bet anything that the people who come to your mind are successful. When I think of examples myself, I even think of young people like Tim Tebow, a quarterback for the Florida Gators. If you are unfamiliar with him, he went on television in the state of Florida following a loss to Ole Miss, and promised that no one would ever see a football player work harder than him to help bring pride to his team. He then followed up what he said with *action*. As a Heisman trophy winner, he led his team to a national championship, and his speech can now be found on the wall of the Florida football facility. His words were inspiring, but he is an inspiration to others because he was motivated himself to *do* exactly what he *said* he would do. Here's Tebow's speech:

> *To the fans and everybody in Gator nation, I'm sorry. I'm extremely sorry. We were hoping for an undefeated season. That was my goal, something that Florida has never done here. I promise you one thing, a lot of good will come out of this. You will never see any player in the entire country play as hard as I will play the rest of the season. You will never see someone push the*

rest of the team as hard as I will push everybody the rest of the season. You will never see a team play harder than we will the rest of the season. God bless.

If you've ever been someone whose actions didn't match your words, that changes today. *You* are now a person who *does everything* that you say you will do. Being motivated for life involves *doing*. Motivation and inspiration without action is worthless. Only when you *do* what you say you will do will you reach your potential.

• Always finish what you start

My greatest God-given ability is my ability to outlast everyone else.
—John Maxwell

Much like the previous key, this one also involves *doing*. Once you start a task or begin pursuing a dream, you have to stick with it until you have accomplished what you want. Even many people who are "doers" forget this important step and move on to a new dream or a new project before the current one is finished. For motivated people, the only time you move on to the next goal is when you have actually accomplished the task at hand. There is no substitute for a good start, but there is also no substitute for a great finish.

For example, I have run multiple marathons in my life. Had I not been committed to finishing what I started, I would have walked away from every single one of them before the race was over. Yet because I was focused on the finish line, I was able to push through the challenges that 26.2 miles present. If you've ever run a marathon, you'll know that the easiest races are the ones with a lot of participants. The reason is that every time you get tired and think about quitting, which will happen at least once, you'll see someone else still running. Their unspoken support in running their own race forces you to evaluate your own capabilities. Additionally, you'll hear encouragement from both the spectators and the runners, which revolves exclusively around finishing. Phrases such as "You're almost there!" and "You can make it!" are the shouts that you'll most often hear. If you talk to marathon runners, you'll find it is a universal truth that the thought of crossing the finish line is what drives people through the mileage. More importantly, the thought of the *feeling* of crossing the finish line is what people strive to achieve.

I often think about the story of a female cross-country athlete at West Virginia University. As you know, a cross-country race is exactly what it implies—a long-distance race across dangerous, uneven, rocky, and often mountainous terrain. One of the female athletes from my school qualified for the NCAA tournament and aspired to achieve All-American status. Unlike such sports as football and basketball, where All-American status is based on yearlong performance, cross-country athletes' dreams of earning the All-American title rest on the outcome of a single race at the NCAA tournament. Being the fastest or slowest runner coming into that single race means absolutely nothing, as the outcome of that single race is the sole determining factor of your status for the year.

In the opening hundred yards of the race, while each of the athletes were jockeying for position, another runner stepped on her foot, and one of her shoes came off. In a race of this magnitude, split seconds can make the difference between being a national champion and merely being a participant. Stopping to put her shoe back on would have taken her to the back of the pack, ruining any chance of achieving her goal. At the same time, going forward meant running the next three miles as fast as she possibly could over rocks and dirt trails. I don't know about you, but I still wince in pain just walking across my parents' gravel driveway without my shoes on. Yet, with the end of the race in mind, she chose to continue the race with one shoe. Focused on the finish line, she earned All-American status, and at the time, was the highest-placing female runner in the history of the WVU program. And she did it all with *one shoe*.

Everyone has a plan, until they get hit. —Evander Holyfield

Any dream worth achieving will come with obstacles. The difference between being good and being great at anything resides in your ability to finish what you start, pressing on in the face of adversity. Once you have established what your ultimate life looks like, your finish line becomes the result of every aspect of your life that you hope to achieve. The cumulative effect of finishing everything that you start will allow you to achieve a motivated life.

Success Strategies

- Always say "please" and "thank you."
- Always show up on time.
- Always do what you say you will do.
- Always finish what you start.
- To achieve success you must follow all four principles all of the time.

Now that you understand the four keys to succeed and are putting them into action, you can anticipate greater success in the future. And additional help in getting more success tomorrow can be found when you start....

Chapter 7

FUTURE SUCCESS FROM YOUR PAST

If you have seen the movie *Searching for Bobby Fisher*, you'll remember the story of a young boy by the name of Josh who was a gifted chess player. The movie was based on a true story about a boy named Josh Waitzkin. Josh was extremely successful at the game of chess, and through his hard work became one of the world's foremost chess players. According to his book, *The Art of Learning*, he became distant from chess and searched for another endeavor in which to place his energy. At the time of his book's release, he was a multiple-time national and world champion in martial arts. In his book, he attempts to explain his process of taking those aspects of his chess-playing life and applying them to martial arts in order to become successful. Now, if you're like me, you should be asking yourself, "How the heck does a world-renowned chess player become a world-class athlete in martial arts?" Those two endeavors would appear to be on opposite ends of the spectrum. However, one of the many things that I learned from his book was how he broke down the various aspects of his chess game and determined which aspects of his game had made him successful. In an interview, he resisted the term "child prodigy." He said that everything he had achieved in the game of chess was because he had put such diligent work into being his best. So this skinny, scrawny chess player took the mental aspects that had made him successful at chess, and used them to excel at martial arts.

Another great example is Jerry Seinfeld. When he was given a comedy award in an HBO special, he spoke about his transition from stand-up comedian, to star of a number-one television show, to stand-up comedian again. He said in his interview that the hardest thing about the transition was taking that "thing" about you that makes you stand out and "pouring it into a different container and having it taste the same." He talked about how hard it was for him to go back to stand-up after having worked on his show for so long, and about how different the two activities really were. Jerry Seinfeld the stand-up comedian had to break down the various successful aspects of himself and his routine, and use those aspects to attain success on his television show. He then had to go back to those same aspects to strengthen his stand-up muscles when he returned to his previous career.

Using Your Gifts

How many times do you see someone who is motivated to be the best at something achieve greatness in another area? Sports stars like Jack Nicklaus and Greg Norman have taken their skills, determination, and work ethic on the golf course to become successful in business. The key is to harness the part of you that has made you great at one thing, and apply that to other areas.

This is something that I've forced myself to do as I've moved through different stages of my life. I was successful in sports because of my work ethic; my competitiveness; my enthusiasm; my willingness to learn; my constant drive to find better coaches and competition; my ability to learn from each and every mistake so that it was not repeated; and my motivation on a daily basis. Once I was finished with sports and moved on to professional school to further my education, I broke down those aspects that had made me successful in the past and used them to excel in the classroom. I shifted my motivation in order to become a hardworking student. I found people to compete with in my classes; I worked to stay excited about my goals; I sought out new information in my field; and I sought out experienced teachers and practitioners. And as I performed better in the classroom, I challenged myself to compete with "smarter" opponents. As with sports, I made errors (more than I would care to admit or remember), but I learned from each mistake and every wrong answer, and made sure that I did not make the same mistake twice. Again, I knew that my ability to stay motivated on a daily basis would put me ahead of 90 percent of the class, so I constantly worked to keep myself fired up!

Going from an individual sport to the classroom was a relatively easy transition for me, because I was still the sole factor in my success. In contrast, moving along to business was not as easy. Going into the business world required more teamwork than I was used to. In reviewing my past, I was forced to explore my leadership qualities and the qualities of those around me. Reviewing my leadership positions in school and in sports, I realized that the times people had followed me were times where my confidence, work ethic, and enthusiasm for reaching my goals had been the clearest. I then took these same aspects and applied them to my business life to help take me, my staff, and my business to the next level.

As I've chosen different areas in which to be motivated, I've constantly reviewed and adapted the core strengths that made me successful in the past. In fact, the whole reason behind writing this book is the enjoyment I take in motivating other people to achieve their goals in various areas of life—as well as my own enjoyment in consistently exploring new areas to become motivated in. The more I've studied the similarities between successful people from completely different areas of life, the more I've found that the common thread is simply being motivated to succeed. Successful people are not necessarily smarter or more talented than everyone else; they simply have made up their minds that they *will* be successful, and then remain motivated on a daily basis to achieve their goals.

Let's apply this to your life today, so that you can start taking action immediately. I want you to think of a time when you experienced success. If multiple successes come to mind, pick the one area in which you have been most successful. Now, I want you to list five personal traits that allowed you to achieve success in that area (be sure to include this list in your Motivational Binder).

My top five personal traits:

1. _____
2. _____
3. _____
4. _____
5. _____

Did you actually write these down? If not, go back and do so before continuing. As you now know, there's a huge difference between *knowing* and *doing*. If you know the answers to these questions but don't actually write them down, then you'll end up doing nothing about them. Remember, the goal of this book is to get you to *do* the things necessary to be your best. Truly motivated people will always write their responses down when they know that they need to.

Now I want you to analyze the area or areas of life where you are currently working to improve. Are you utilizing all five of these personal gifts to help you achieve your potential? I'll bet that you aren't... yet!

Now, for each of those personal gifts that are not being fully utilized to help you achieve your potential in current areas, I want you to list three ways in which you can better use these gifts (be sure to include this list in your Motivational Binder).

Underutilized Gift 1: _____

Ways which I can maximize this gift to achieve my potential in current areas:

1. _____
2. _____
3. _____

Gift 2: _____

Ways which I can maximize this gift to achieve my potential in current areas:

1. _____
2. _____
3. _____

Gift 3: _____

Ways which I can maximize this gift to achieve my potential in current areas:

1. _____
2. _____
3. _____

Success Strategies

- What core strengths have made you successful in the past?
- To reach your highest success, maximize your strengths.
- How could you use your strengths in each of your *be, do,* and *have* goals to achieve success?
- What strengths do you need to develop to achieve greater success?
- Successful people are ordinary people who have made up their minds to be successful.

Some of the same traits that you have listed here are also most likely found in....

Lessons from Everest

One day, while scrolling through the channels, I came upon a life-changing documentary on the Discovery Channel about climbers who successfully made it to the top of Mount Everest. The documentary began by describing, in excruciating detail, the numerous unsuccessful attempts that had been made to climb Mount Everest. Unlike many of life's challenges, an unsuccessful climb up Mount Everest often leads to death, rather than mere disappointment. As they revealed details about many of the attempts, they showed that, for hundreds of years, many of our planet's most physically and mentally tough people had made the decision to climb Everest. They prepared for their journey by going through exhaustive physical training, often simulating climbs with their full backpack gear strapped on. Visualization techniques were also used to mentally prepare for the journey. Climbing Mount Everest is not merely a hike. It is a test of the human spirit. These people were testing themselves against physical exhaustion, severe terrain, drastic weather changes, significant oxygen deficits due to the altitude, and mental agony. All of these people put their lives on hold and risked their very being to attempt to climb the great mountain. Although they were in peak physical and mental shape for the test, centuries went by before anyone made it to the top.

The early attempts were very similar in nature. Most were made by single individuals, rather than groups or teams, so that the climbers could go at their own pace, stopping when they were fatigued, and pushing on when they felt motivated. Their plans of attack were also very similar; their roadmaps basically called for them to go straight up the mountain, constantly pressing to get to the next checkpoint. At best, these attempts failed, and the climbers simply turned around and went back down the mountain. At worst, the climbers not only failed to reach the top, they also didn't make it to the bottom.

According to the documentary, a team finally came into the picture with a new plan. Instead of attempting to climb individually, they decided to go as a team. They also changed the game plan for climbing. Rather than constantly moving up the mountain from checkpoint to checkpoint, they theorized that the early failures were due to the human body's lack of acclimation to the thin air at the higher altitudes. Their plan called for slowly working their way up the mountain in a diagonal fashion from one checkpoint to the next, often stopping for days at a time to allow their bodies to adjust. They even planned to backtrack down the mountain to previous checkpoints to allow their bodies brief breaks from the higher altitudes, before moving back up the mountain to the next few checkpoints.

The result is that they developed a successful model for reaching the peak of the mountain. Now, anyone attempting to climb the mountain follows the same basic outline that this team used. Plans may vary in terms of rest point locations, timing, and team size, but the same basic outline for success is always there, including the temporary backtracking down the mountain before moving another two checkpoints ahead.

Now let's apply the lessons from Everest to our own lives. When it comes to living a truly motivated life, don't aim for anything smaller than you are capable of achieving. Don't attempt to climb a molehill when you could conquer the highest mountain if you decided to.

Success in anything is *not* random. The team that eventually conquered the mountain had a well-thought-out game plan, and they stuck to it. Preparation is one of the keys to achieving any goal. If you're going to climb any mountain, you can't show up at the base one-day and decide to start the climb. You must know what you want to do, plan your strategy for achieving it, and prepare for success as thoroughly as possible.

Success is never linear. Like the individuals who failed to climb Mount Everest by attempting to go straight up the mountain, we often head in one direction without taking the time to plan our "checkpoints" along the way. The successful team moved up the mountain in a methodical, diagonal approach, still moving forward, but not exceeding their physical or mental capabilities.

Success often requires you to take one step back before taking many steps forward. The climbers intentionally planned out their regression to earlier checkpoints before moving back up to even greater heights. With your goals in life, you must be prepared for setbacks. Temporary setbacks should be seen as just that—temporary! In business, in sports, and in life, they are essential for us to ultimately learn, grow, and achieve our goals.

Success does not have to be a lonely process. Where the individuals failed in the early attempts, the team prevailed. Teams allow you to pull from each other's strengths. If you are trying to achieve your goals alone, I strongly urge you to find someone to go on the journey with you *today*. One plus one does *not* equal two; two people attempting to achieve the same goal together are exponentially greater than the individual alone.

Success does not require you to reinvent the wheel. Since the initial, successful model has been established, climbers have consistently followed that same basic trip outline. The exact game plan may be refined or modified, but the basic outline is still intact. Similarly, for almost anything that you are trying to accomplish, you can find someone who's been successful at it already. And if you're truly doing something that's never been attempted before, look outside your area, find someone who has been equally as successful in another endeavor, and follow their basic outline for success. Too often, we spend our days whining and complaining, thinking that "nobody understands" or that "no one has ever gone through this before." All the while, someone either is, or has already been, successful at what we're trying to achieve. Find them. Find their books. Find their friends. Find out how they did it!

Success in anything is a journey that you have to make yourself. While successful climbers worked as a team to reach the top of Mount Everest, no one could complete the climb for them. You can't devise a plan and then send someone else up the mountain; you've got to do it yourself. Part of reaching the top in anything is the journey itself, and knowing at the end that *you* did it! A mentor of mine often says, "You have to do it yourself— and you can't do it alone." Whatever you're trying to achieve, you need to know that no one is ever going to do it for you. Get a team in place to help you along the way, but you'll ultimately be responsible for your own success! And not only will you be responsible for your own success, you will also be responsible for creating your *own* Mount Everest. I hope the following poem inspires you on your journey:

The Hill

But then comes the Hill and I know that I am made for more.
And by becoming more, I am challenged to choose suffering,
to endure pain, and to bear hardship.

At first the gentle swell carries me… but gradually
the Hill demands more and more. I have reached the end
of what is possible. Now it is beyond what I can stand.
The temptation is to say, "Enough! This much is enough."
But I will not give in.

I am fighting God. Fighting the limitations He gave me.
Fighting the pain. Fighting the unfairness. Fighting all t
he evil in me and the world. And I will not give in. I will
conquer this Hill, and I will conquer it alone.

—George Sheehan

Success Strategies

- Choose goals that are worthy of your abilities.
- You must decide what you want, plan your strategy for success, and prepare as thoroughly as possible.
- Two people attempting to achieve the same goal are exponentially greater than an individual alone.
- Success does not require you to reinvent the wheel.
- Success in anything is a journey that you must make yourself.

Chapter 8

SUCCESS BEYOND EXPECTATIONS

Now that you've decided which aspects of life you wish to improve, and have broken down each aspect into smaller pieces to conquer incrementally, you'll need to place your improvement strategies on a timeline.

Timeline

My recommendation is that you first look at where you want to be one year from now and five years from now, then fill out a one and five-year plan in each respective category (be sure to include this list in your Motivational Binder).

<u>One Year:</u>

Be:

1. _____

2. _____

3. _____

Do:

1. _____
2. _____
3. _____

Have:

1. _____
2. _____
3. _____

<u>Five Years</u>

Be:

1. _____
2. _____
3. _____

Do:

1. _____
2. _____
3. _____

Have:

1. _____
2. _____
3. _____

Once this list is complete, you should review it at the beginning and end of each day. You'll find yourself making better decisions about how you spend your time. If daily activities do not fall in line with your purpose and with your immediate goals, then they are not worthy of your time.

Unless you begin with the end in mind, you'll never get there. It is essential that you give yourself a deadline for completing every dream you have. Once you've come up with a scheduled deadline, you can then break down the timeline in the same way you broke down the goals themselves.

A five-year plan can be broken down into smaller, one-year increments. One-year increments can be broken down into quarterly goals. Quarterly goals can be broken into monthly goals. Monthly goals can be broken into weekly goals. Weekly goals can be broken down into daily goals. And at this point, you are now familiar with the importance of *today*!

I believe that setting timelines is the only way to ensure that you reach your goals. If you bypass this step, you'll continually find yourself in the "someday" form of thinking:

- "Someday I'll have…"
- "Someday I'll do…"
- "Someday I'll be…."

Without a deadline, your "someday" will become a "never"! Set a time for things to happen, and then stick to it. With a timeline, your "someday" will be clearly defined with a date, and you'll know exactly when you'll *be, do,* and *have* everything on your list.

A college professor of mine spoke extensively about his "work-retire" philosophy. He pointed out that most people work their entire lives thinking that they'll have plenty of time for doing what they *really* want to do once they retire. My professor, however, noticed that many of these people worked for dreams that never took place. As a solution to this problem, he suggested determining what it was that you want, putting it on a definite timeline, and completing it as soon as possible so that you can move on to the next dream. Rather than working your life away, hoping that you'll one day reach a point where you can *be, do,* and *have* all of the things you want, set up a timeline for each individual goal so that you can enjoy these things along the journey. Instead of thinking about life in two separate phases, work and retirement, start thinking about work and the retired lifestyle as simultaneous. You can work hard and enjoy the luxuries of retirement at the *same* time by doing the things now that bring joy to your life.

Another question that I pose to myself and others is, "Where will you be in a year from now?" You'll either be better or worse, but you won't be the same. We should all aim to be better at everything in a year from now. Again, I've seen too many people in sports, in business, and in life who believe that, once they get to a certain level, they can just coast their way through life, putting things on autopilot. But again, no person, no business, and no team will ever remain the same for any period of time. You will either be better or worse, but never the same. So inevitably, those who try to "maintain" their level will be worse, because they're placing no effort and no energy into getting better. In contrast, if you're following my recommendations and working to get better each and every day, you'll find that effort and energy are in endless supply. Utilizing each moment as effectively and efficiently as possible will bring you closer to achieving your motivated life, and as you make progress, you'll find yourself feeling more energized every step of the way.

Another bonus of setting timelines is that you'll begin to place more value on your time. When you are motivated for life, you'll find yourself using every second in the most productive way possible. Regardless of which goal you are currently working toward, being motivated to be your best in all aspects will require a better use of your time. Think about how much time you waste right now on things that have nothing to do with living your dream life. How much time do you waste watching TV, surfing the net each day, or even driving to and from work? If you were to take this extra time and use it for one or more of the many areas in which you wish to improve, you will quickly begin to realize all of your goals. You'll find that people who are motivated for life will hold their time as one of their most precious gifts. You won't find a motivated person wasting time when there are goals to achieve. I urge you to analyze your day right now and see if there aren't moments when you can gain back some precious time. Once you've found where this extra time will come from, make sure that you fill that time only with productive activities—activities that will bring you closer to all of the items on your *be, do, have* list.

> *I resolve to live with all my might while I do live. I resolve never to lose one moment of time and to improve my use of time in the most profitable way I possibly can. I resolve never to do anything I wouldn't do if it were the last hour of my life.* —Dr. Bruce Wilkinson

Success Strategies

- Define what you want to *be, do,* and *have* in one year and in five years from now.

- Every dream must be given a deadline for completion.

- Without a timeline to complete your goals, "someday" will become a "never."

- Where will you be in a year from now? You'll either be better or worse, since nothing stays the same.

- Use every second of your day in the most productive ways possible. You do *not* have all the time in the world to achieve your dreams.

When you do, you will begin to achieve....

Exponential Growth

If you read any business books, listen to any business audio series, or go to any business seminars, you'll find a common theme. They'll teach you how to grow your business by doing one of three things. You either grow the number of clients, the number of time the clients return, or the total amount that each client spends when doing business with you. These three aspects run every business. All of the other procedures that every business must constantly perform are essentially done in an effort to grow these three main aspects of the business. You don't advertise simply for the sake of advertising; you're trying to grow your number of new clients. You don't complete daily business procedures just for the sake of doing them; you're trying to promote repeat business. You're not offering ancillary services just for the customer's convenience; rather, you're trying to grow the amount of money that each client spends that particular day. Get the idea? Businesses work extremely hard to intentionally grow these numbers through new campaigns and strategies. Having attended many business seminars, I have heard business owners state their goals for the upcoming year as "growing our number of new clients by 10 percent." Others implement marketing strategies to encourage past customers to return and set such goals as "increasing retention by 10 percent." Often these strategies are successful, and they achieve single-digit increase in their bottom line, or, if they are ultra successful, they may achieve a full 10 percent growth. However, the exciting part is when you go to work on all three aspects *at the same time*. If you were to grow your business by 10 percent in each area, you would essentially grow the business by a third! Even if you were to fall short of all three of your goals, you would still likely achieve 20 percent growth in your business. Again, the goal merely switched from focusing on only one aspect of business growth, to focusing on all three aspects to expand exponentially. Instead of looking at the overall picture and saying that you would like to grow by 30 percent or more, you just focus on making minor changes to each of the three smaller areas, and they culminate to create a huge result. Another special hint about this process is that, if you truly want 30 percent growth, you should work the numbers to shoot for 40 percent instead. This will give you a little wiggle room for unforeseen challenges in one or more of these areas, yet still give you reasonable expectations for achieving your goals.

Now let's apply this to your life. What aspects of your life need to be motivated to expand? Let me give you some hints. You are probably one, or many, of the following: a son, daughter, husband, wife, brother, sister, friend, employee, employer, coach, athlete, teacher, student, etc. The list goes on and on. We're all wearing several different hats throughout the day. Let's initially just focus on three different aspects and work to grow them by 10 percent each. Chances are that you probably picked up this book, or were given it as a gift, because you were extremely motivated— or need to be—to change and expand one specific aspect of your life. Let's take this opportunity to not only expand in that one area, but also in other areas that may directly or indirectly affect that aspect as well.

When you are dealing with expanding your life, versus expanding your business, you're at a disadvantage when it comes to quantifying your results. However, this exercise will still apply, and I promise you that if you follow through with writing down and then improving three areas, you'll feel the cumulative result—and it will often exceed the 30 percent example above. Now, in each of these three areas, list five specific actions that you will take to increase your success in that area (and be sure to include this in your Motivational Binder).

Aspect 1: _____

1. _____
2. _____
3. _____
4. _____
5.. _____

Aspect 2: _____

1. _____
2. _____
3. _____
4. _____
5.. _____

Aspect 3: _____

1. _____

2. _____

3. _____

4. _____

5.. _____

To get you going, here's an example of how I'd fill out one of these aspects in my personal life:

Aspect 1: Father

1. Read to my child ten minutes every night

2. Plan special "father activity" once a month

3. Tell my child that I love them at least ten times each day

4. Keep a daily journal of my child's successes

5. Tell my child at least once a day how great their mother is

The point is that, if you want to truly live a motivated life, you must get motivated in all aspects and raise expectations in everything you do. You cannot have a motivated business life if you do not have a motivated life outside of work. Likewise, you cannot have a motivated personal life and be uninspired at work. If you want to improve your athletic skills, work to improve as a leader. If you want to improve your marriage, improve your motivation at work. Let's motivate every single aspect of your life. That is what you want, isn't it? Life is moving more quickly each day, so start living the motivated life that you deserve today.

Success Strategies

- Make minor changes to multiple areas of life in order to produce huge results.

- Choose to improve in *every* area of your life.

- Raise your expectations in everything that you can *be, do,* and *have.*

- Successful people have both a great work life and a great personal life.

- You *can* have it all.

Chapter 9

THE WINNER'S EDGE

You don't have to pick and choose one or two things to which to dedicate your life. I have found that the people who are truly motivated for life have learned that they can have it all. The key is learning to find the perfect....

Balance

Some of the best advice that I've ever received in sports also translates into great advice for life in general. Former NCAA wrestling champion Scott Collins told me early in my collegiate career that, "there is a time for everything. There is a time for family, a time for friends, a time to learn, a time to teach, and a time to compete. When you can find that perfect balance, that's when you'll be successful." I've found that advice essential to gaining a better understanding of my responsibilities in sports. However, as life has progressed, I've found his advice to hold true in all areas, be it in sports, in school, in marriage, in business, or in life in general.

In order for you to maximize your potential to be motivated for life, you have to master all aspects of your life. The real issue is that you cannot lie to yourself. If you're working so hard to achieve your athletic goals that you neglect your schoolwork, you can't lie to yourself about it. Now, you may justify it in your mind, but you'll know deep down that you're not doing your best. If you're working so hard to achieve your business and financial goals that it comes at the expense of your family, you'll know it. Again, maybe you'll choose to justify it in one way or another, or maybe you'll choose to ignore your challenges, but you cannot lie to yourself.

The motivated life is a balanced life. It is one in which you consistently work to be the best you can be at each individual aspect of your life, every single day.

It is truly difficult to bring down a person who is motivated for life. When you give the best that you have and receive great things in return, the stumbling blocks that you may run into will seem much smaller. For instance, if a sport were the only thing in life in which you were truly motivated to be your best, what would happen if you lost? What would happen if you had an injury that kept you out of that sport for a significant amount of time? What would happen if you didn't make the cut? If you only give significance to one area of your life, it's a major blow when you hit a bump in the road in that single area. However, when you're motivated to be your best at every aspect of your life, a bump in the road is just that—a bump. Your own self-worth never drops, because you're still the same motivated person. A person who sees themselves solely as a motivated athlete will be easily demoralized when they lose. A person who sees themselves as motivated for life will analyze their loss, correct what was within their control, and move on to being a motivated friend, a motivated student, a motivated teammate, a motivated family member, and so forth.

Being motivated in more areas does not diminish the importance of what you may go through in any one area, but will allow you to skip over the breaks in the path and keep a healthy perspective on the importance (or unimportance) of stumbling blocks in your way. When you're motivated about everything you do and have a purpose that is "others focused," you'll never allow your own self-worth or confidence to be damaged due to a small blow in one area.

I often think about a statement made by Lloyd Carr, former coach of the Michigan football team. As you may or may not know, the Michigan football tradition is extremely important to fans both state- and nationwide. Its tradition of excellence requires nothing short of greatness from its team members. Early in the 2007 season, Michigan lost a game to Appalachian State, a team that was merely seen as a warm-up to get Michigan ready for the rest of their season with elite Big 10 teams. It was considered one of the biggest David and Goliath upsets of football history. Shortly thereafter, Michigan lost again to Michigan State.

Given the enormous expectations and a football history filled with success, many of the supporters and university faculty members began to call for Coach Carr's resignation. Coach Carr, who had a reputation for leading an extraordinary life off the football field, was asked in an interview about his plans to continue the season after devastating losses and calls for his resignation. He replied, "Nothing can get me down! Not a loss to Appalachian State, not a loss to Michigan State, not the loss of my job. Nothing can get me down!"

To me, this statement is the epitome of living a motivated life. Having balance in your life and being motivated to be the best at all that you do will give you this mentality. Even potentially major catastrophes will be seen as tremendous, and nothing will be able to get you down.

That said it's often difficult to find this balance. For my part, I still feel as if I'm constantly working to find a better balance between different areas of my life. Priorities change as life goes on, especially once you have a family of your own. But recognizing the importance of a balanced life, identifying the areas that need to be balanced, and then applying the proper amount of effort to each will ensure that your life is always the best one that you can live.

The fun part is that a snowball effect will eventually begin to take place. Once you realize the importance of having a balanced life, you'll find your successes from one area starting to carry over into other areas as well. You'll gain strength, confidence, and momentum from being good at work, and that will carry over into your marriage. You'll gain strength, confidence, and momentum from being your best in the classroom, and that will carry over into your friendships. Simply focus your energy at all times on getting and giving the most to life that you have to offer, pay attention to the importance of a balanced life, and before you know it, you'll have the life you've always wanted in all aspects.

Success Strategies

- There is a time for everything in life.

- Choose to balance out your daily routine so that you can reach your optimum success.

- You can't lie to yourself. Only you know if you are doing your best in each area of life.

- When your life is balanced, stumbling blocks will appear much smaller and more temporary.

- In a balanced life, catastrophes become opportunities.

All of this can be accomplished with minor improvements in each individual category. This is best demonstrated by the....

Success Bell Curve

*Every successful person finds that great success lies
just beyond the point where they're convinced the
idea is not going to work.* —Napoleon Hill

Being motivated for life requires becoming as successful as you can possibly be in every area of your life. One of my most influential college professors, Dr. Stiller, one day drew what he called the "Success Bell Curve" for our class. As an engineer, Dr. Stiller has been responsible for several innovative patents on various mechanical and environmental ideas, so this principle was essential in helping him to be persistent enough to reach a finished product with each experiment. The following illustration shows what he believed to be the difference between success and failure.

SUCCESS BELL CURVE

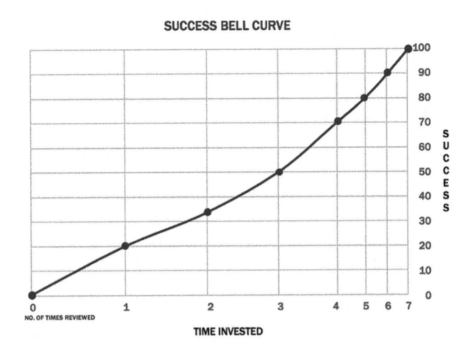

NO. OF TIMES REVIEWED

TIME INVESTED

As you will see, this is what Dr. Stiller believed to be the path to success. The numbers on the vertical line indicate the level of success, while the numbers at the bottom represent time and effort. Dr. Stiller originally used this graph to explain how to study. As Dr. Stiller explained, you typically will learn the material gradually as you read through your notes. On the first time, reading each word of your notes takes a lot of time and will produce very little results, as your retention will be minimal. As you read through the notes a second time, you begin to go through them more quickly and recall many of the lines that you have already read. With each additional reading, the time to complete your notes will lessen, while your retention goes up. Now draw your attention to the right part of the bell curve, specifically, the sharp spike at the end. As you'll see, this last part is where all of the success occurs. Most people will read through their notes four to five times, which in Dr. Stiller's estimation, will take up most of the available time at the bottom of the graph. However, this will only produce a mediocre result, often a score of 70–80 percent. Those who read through their notes an additional two to three times will only expend an extra 10 percent in time and effort, yet that effort will result in a 20–30 percent increase in their scores.

Upon learning this, I began to follow his advice, and found it to be absolutely true. Instead of reading through my notes four to five times and earning a B or C like everyone else in the class, I began to put in the extra 10 percent effort by reading through my notes at least seven times before each test. Without exaggeration, until that point I'd studied 90 percent as long and hard, but was only able to earn Bs and Cs. Once I began doing this, I excelled in the classroom. As a result, not only was I honored as a First Team Academic All-American in college, but I also gained Summa Cum Laude honors en route to my doctorate degree. I tell you this not to brag, but to let you in on this tiny secret to my success. I went from mediocre to the top of the class, simply because I applied this rule.

I have found this same rule to hold true in virtually every aspect of life. Most people are so busy working hard for mediocre results that they never put in that additional 10 percent effort that would lead to a 20–30 percent increase in their productivity. What you need to realize is that 95 percent of the population does not give that extra 10 percent effort that would lead them to the life of their dreams. I have found that, without exception, those who are motivated for life consistently apply 10 percent more effort to everything that they do. They realize the importance of that one extra step. By doing this, they not only enjoy more success in their ability to *be, do,* and *have* everything that they want, but they also know that the small amount of additional effort involved removes 95 percent of the competition, who will naturally quit too early.

In the *The 4-Hour Work Week*, Timothy Ferriss states:

> *Ninety-nine percent of people in the world are convinced they are incapable of achieving great things, so they aim for the mediocre. The level of competition is thus fiercest for "realistic" goals, paradoxically making them the most time and energy consuming. It is easier to raise $10,000,000 than it is $1,000,000. It is easier to pick up the one perfect 10 in the bar than the five 8's.*

If you are insecure, guess what? The rest of the world is, too. Do not overestimate the competition and underestimate yourself. You are better than you think.[2]

Years ago, a friend related a story to me that he thought I could appreciate. As I pass it on to you, I stress that, while the numbers are both outdated and have not been checked for their exact accuracy, the point of the story remains unchanged.

My friend worked for a shipping company and set up a meeting with a representative selling a product. The representative believed his product would increase the shipping company's efficiency by 5 percent. Upon hearing the price of the product, my friend told the representative that he planned to pass on the offer, feeling that the measly 5 percent did not justify the expense. At this point, the representative replied, "Sir, can I ask you a question? Can you tell me what $350,000 represents?"

My friend replied, "No."

"$350,000 represents the average amount earned last year by a professional golfer on the PGA Tour. Now let me ask you another question. Can you tell me what $9 million represents?"

My friend replied, "No."

"$9 million represents how much Tiger Woods earned last year on the PGA Tour. Now let me ask you one more question. Can you tell me what 5 percent represents?"

My friend once again replied, "No."

The salesman said, "Five percent represents how much more accurate Tiger Woods' golf shots are in comparison to the average golfer on the PGA Tour."

Again, while the accuracy of these numbers may not be exact, you get the point. A slight amount of additional effort will lead to extraordinary

---

2   Timothy Ferriss, *The 4-Hour Workweek*, 50.

results. And as we covered in the section on exponential growth, a small amount of additional effort in multiple aspects of your life will lead to exponential results in your life as a whole.

The most common trait I have found in all successful people is that they have conquered the temptation to give up. —Peter Lowe

Success Strategies

- Additional efforts of only 10 percent often produce a 20–30 percent increase in productivity.

- Ninety-five percent of the population never puts in the extra 10 percent effort to achieve the life of their dreams.

- In competitive settings, most people give up way too soon.

- The larger your goals, the fewer competitors you'll face.

- Successful people always apply 10 percent more effort than everyone else to everything they do.

Begin right now to add that extra 10 percent effort to every area of your life. The extra effort will yield immediate results when you apply it because....

Chapter 10

NOW IS THE TIME

A ll too often, we go through events in life without working to maximize our potential today. We put off important tasks and decisions, or even worse, let someone else handle them. In sports and in business, I've been more successful than most, simply because I was motivated to push myself to a higher level each and every day. Success in any endeavor is as simple as having a great *today*.

Again, the goal is not necessarily to be the best, but rather to be *your* best. Recognition typically goes to the ones who stand out from the crowd and are better than others at their given endeavors. That said if you were to speak to some of these successful people, you'd find that they are typically focused on being *their* best, not on "standing out." Trying to be the best that you can be on a daily basis is enough to push you to greatness. If you look at the Donald Trumps of the business world or the Tiger Woods of the sports world, you'll find a common theme—they are all considered great at what they do, not because of one special tournament or one spectacular deal, but rather because of the total body of their work. At the same time, their extraordinary body of work is special because of the motivated decisions and actions that they took on a daily basis to achieve their own potential. You'll never see an athlete who hasn't put in motivated, daily efforts just show up and win a sporting event. You'll never see a businessman who hasn't put in motivated, daily efforts to perfect his craft just walk in and close a multi-million-dollar deal. These things happen because motivated, daily efforts accumulate to create a great week, and motivated weeks combine to create a motivated year. Continuously motivated years produce extraordinary bodies of work. As Lao-tzu said, "A journey of a thousand miles begins with the first step." What could you do right now, at this very moment, to move closer to being the best you that you could be today? If you're constantly working to be your best each and every moment, you'll have no time for stress or worries in your life. Staying focused on being a motivated person in every aspect of your life puts all of your energy in a positive direction.

One of the keys to these efforts is having a list of priorities in front of you to guide you through your day, so that you keep first things first and stay motivated in the proper areas. After you've prioritized the different aspects of your motivated life, you must then recognize which aspects you are currently living at this moment, so that you can follow your priorities. For example, if you're at work for the day, you're in the role of a motivated worker. After your day is done and you get back to your home, you may need to switch to the role of motivated father, mother, or spouse. By having a list of preset priorities, you can always establish which hat you should be wearing.

To give you an example, my list of priorities is as follows:

- God
- Wife
- Kids
- Family
- Friends
- Leading/Teaching
- Work
- Fitness.

Having those priorities in place allows me to make better decisions about how to handle daily events and determine where the bulk of my motivation should go. If I want to get my workout in for the day, but still have work that needs to be done, I place being a motivated worker in the top-priority position, and complete that work before moving on to the exercise. If I'm working but my daughter is home from school and wants to play, I know that I must put the work on hold and go into motivated father mode.

These different roles will obviously be different for everyone, but defining all of the different roles that you play on a daily basis, prioritizing those roles, then reviewing your priorities daily will keep you on track to staying motivated in the right areas. I read through my list every single day, and have done so for the past several years. I know that if I don't review my priorities daily, I'll start putting my motivation into the wrong areas. What good would it be for me to be the ultimate, motivated worker, but to neglect my family as an unmotivated father or husband? If you don't prioritize and repeatedly review your priorities, you'll get lost in the repetitiveness of life. If your ultimate goal is to truly be your best, these priorities must be followed every day.

Just as in the previous example, the truly motivated life is the result of working in each area of your life at the proper time and on a consistent basis. The best *you* possible is available right now; just follow the steps, and get to work!

> *Today can be a day to remember.*
> *You can make it so. Today is yours to do with as you see fit.*
> *You can use it, delight in it, accomplish as much as your capabilities permit, and enjoy today to the fullest.*
> *Use a portion of today's 24 hours in a helpful way.*
> *Spend a part of today's 1440 minutes in meaningful meditation.*
> *Share some of today's 86,400 seconds in service to others.*
> *Today will soon disappear. Make the most of it; for once it passes, its opportunities will never return again.*
> *If you take time each day to pray, play, work, laugh, love profusely, and to thank God will all your heart, you will always have a day to remember.*

—Virginia J. Ruehlmann

Success Strategies

- Successful people are motivated each and every day to be their best.

- Motivated daily effort accumulates to create a great week, and motivated weeks create an extraordinary year.

- What could you do right this minute to move closer to your goals?

- Define your various roles in life, prioritize them, and review them daily.

- Established priorities direct your daily decisions.

The tricky part of achieving your ultimate success is learning that, while success does lie in a great today, you must also learn to....

Sacrifice the Now

It's smart to defer gratification. Indeed, deferring gratification is a good definition of being civilized. Take less at first in order to get much more later. —Bernice Fitz-Gibbon

Being motivated for life will often require you to sacrifice the "now." What I mean by this is that, by working to your capacity today and delaying your reward until later, you'll receive a much greater end result. Regardless of which aspects of life you choose to alter as a result of reading this book, you've got to be prepared to sacrifice the now.

We've already learned about the importance of "today." Living and giving everything that you possibly can to each "today" is the only way you will ever come close to reaching your potential. However, that does not mean that you will *have, be,* and *do* all of the things that you want to achieve immediately. This is a tricky concept, but one that I've found every successful person must follow. On one hand, I'm telling you that you must get and give everything you have to your life *today* in order to live the life of your dreams right now. On the other hand, I'm telling you that you must learn to sacrifice the now in order to achieve an even better life tomorrow. I believe that it is not only possible to do both, but also essential if you plan to truly live a motivated life.

As an example, let's look at athletes. Do you know any athletes who've been able to skip all the training, show up for competition, and be at their best? It doesn't happen. All successful athletes know that by working to their capacity each and every day, they'll eventually be able to achieve their highest level later. Even the highest-level athletes know that you can't have everything right now. You can't wake up one day, decide to win the Heisman Trophy, and accomplish that dream by the end of the day. It just isn't going to happen. It takes years and years of hard work and discipline to ever achieve a dream that big. Yet every single college football player striving for that accomplishment is willing to put in the work necessary to be his best today, in hopes of winning the trophy later.

To again reference Tiger Woods, here's an interesting tidbit: several years ago, while ranked the number-one golfer in the world, he decided to change his golf swing. Why would the number-one golfer in the world want to change his swing? He's the best in the world! But Tiger felt that, in order to be *his* best, he needed to change his mechanics. He sacrificed his game and his international ranking at that time, in order to make changes that would make him an even stronger golfer later. Most people at the top of the sport would not be willing to make such changes. They would want to keep everything just as it was and try to repeat what was working. But motivated athletes who know they can do better do what it takes and *sacrifice the now* in order to become *their* best later.

Again, you say, "I already know that! This is a simple concept." I agree. However, while it may be simple and you do probably already *know* and believe this concept, I care about what you *do*. My observations of most people have led me to conclude that people do not follow this rule. Look at the number of people who go on a diet, only to give up after a day or two because they haven't yet reached their goal weight. Or, look at the New Year's resolutions people make about exercise. Go to the local gym the first Monday after the New Year, and I'll guarantee you it'll be packed with people trying to slim down. However, if you go back merely one month later, you'll find that the gyms are back down to their normal population again. I believe that everyone who originally went to the gym had good intentions and really did want to lose weight and get in better shape. However, most people look in the mirror after a few days of exercise, and when they see no change, they conclude that the exercise wasn't working and quit. Is this really the case? Was the exercise really not working? Of course not! It's just that it takes a certain amount of time and repetition to create a physical change. But for most people, if the instant gratification isn't there, then they won't do what is necessary to stick to a plan.

As another example, let's look at finances. Everyone wants to be rich, but no one wants to work harder to make more money, or save that money in order to invest it properly for tomorrow's prosperity. Everyone just wants to make money today, spend it today, and complain about those who have more than they do. Having met many so-called "rich" people, I can tell you that 99 percent of them have had to make tremendous sacrifices in order to get where they are today. Remember this, and do what they have done, rather than being jealous of their success.

What you must remember is that, just because you haven't achieved everything that you dream of achieving yet, that doesn't mean that life, still can't be incredible today! There truly is joy in the journey. Everything that you want in life can be found in the *quest* of achieving your potential. The end product will be worth the wait, but for the motivated life, working *toward* that big goal is everything.

To use a few examples from my own life, I can tell you that, as a wrestler, I made a lot of sacrifices. While many of my friends were out goofing off, I was training. While everyone else was relaxing during the summer, I was training. While everyone was going on extravagant spring break trips in college, I was training. In the end, I was more successful, because I trained more than everyone else. But here's the neat thing about it—I enjoyed training. I never felt as though I missed out on anything as a result of training, but rather, I feel that others missed out on the success that I was fortunate enough to enjoy because they were not focused on a goal.

Likewise, I've found that, as a coach, I also have to sacrifice the "now." I've been in the same boat that most coaches find themselves in: while we have a lot to show our athletes, we all know that we must start with the basics. A lot of the technique that we coaches *could* show would be more fun and more creative than the basics, but we all know that the basics are essential building blocks for moving on to bigger and better things. We know we must stick to the basics until they are perfected, before we can enjoy the bigger successes of more elaborate technique.

In business, I've also followed in the steps of many other successful businessmen and have had to sacrifice a lot in order to get where I am today. Many people will look at a business like mine and say, "I want what you have." But are you willing to do what I had to do to get it? During chiropractic school, I had a very modest lifestyle, since I was supported by financial aid and by my wife, who worked throughout my education. Six months after graduating and opening my own practice, I found myself producing a small profit. At that point, most people would have spent the money immediately, feeling entitled after having endured such a limited lifestyle during school. However, following the advice and instruction of others with successful practices, I put every bit of money toward debt reduction and back into the business. At the end of each month, I calculated the profit, then invested that money into new equipment, advertising, and staff so that I could bring the business to a higher level. To this day, many of my staff members do not realize that they were taking home a paycheck well before I ever did. It was nearly two years before I began taking any of the profit for my family's personal use. But because I was able to delay gratification until later and sacrifice the "now," my personal paychecks ended up being much greater, because I had grown the business to a level that produced much more profit. There were many times during those first two years that I wanted to write myself a check, and even times when I felt that I needed the money, but I also knew that paying the price of investing back into the business would pay huge dividends in the end.

These personal examples aren't unique to me; they're typical of those living a motivated life. When you begin to review your goals on a daily basis, remember that it's okay if you're not there yet. Stay focused on being your best each day, and you'll eventually get whatever it is that you wish to obtain.

Even if your new, motivated life includes becoming a better person in general, you need to remember that transformations don't happen overnight. We are all flawed. We'll continue to make mistakes every single day, without exception. However, if you decide that you're going to become a better person and begin to apply the principles and instructions from this book to help you get there, your life can change today. But obviously, you also need to give yourself some time. The person you're capable of becoming will take some work.

Patience is the key element of success. —Bill Gates

This brings us to the next topic....

Patience

You miss 100 percent of the shots that you don't take. —Wayne Gretzky

As I see it, patience is a tricky concept. It creates a dilemma similar to the one of working to your capacity *today*, while at the same time sacrificing the now. Hopefully, I can shed some light on it.

If you have set goals that are beyond your reach, then you'll need to develop the virtue of patience. No goals worth achieving are going to happen overnight; they must be nurtured and cultivated daily in order to reap the greater benefits tomorrow. I've found that most people leading a motivated life struggle with this virtue more than anything else. I certainly know that I have. Once you've determined what your motivated life will look like, it's possible to live that life *today*, but you won't necessarily reap the benefits of that life until later. You must have patience to wait for the benefits, but find joy in the act of living a motivated life, in which you get and give everything to life *today*.

Here's where the tricky part comes in. You need to develop patience, but at the same time, you must also *expect* success. And the sooner you *expect* to be successful, the sooner that you *will* be successful. I learned this principle from a friend of mine named Greg Jones. Greg was also a wrestler, and went through the same collegiate program that I did a few years after I had graduated. But we had very different experiences in that program. During my college career, I always knew that being a NCAA champion was a goal that I could potentially accomplish someday, on the basis of my successful high school career. However, I was also willing to accept the patience it would require before I could possibly reach that goal. And just as I had thought, by my senior year, I was in a position to compete for the title.

Now let's look at my friend Greg. Greg completed his high school career on a very good note, winning the Pennsylvania State Championship. But as he entered college, Greg's expectations for himself were much greater than mine. Where I saw my first few years of my collegiate career as a necessary evil to attain eventual success, he saw the possibility of immediate success. He was willing to put in the necessary work. And at the end of his freshman year, he achieved every collegiate athlete's goal: he became an NCAA champion. It didn't happen randomly—he expected it! Moreover, I'm sure that, even if Greg hadn't experienced immediate success, he would have shown the necessary patience to become not only his best, but *the* best.

I often remarked that, while Greg had amazing physical gifts, if you were to put his brain in another body, he would still have been successful, because he expected success and then backed up his expectations with action. His mind told him that *immediate* success was possible, and because of that, he *immediately* began to train and compete as if he were going to experience immediate success. Greg Jones completed his collegiate career as a three-time NCAA champion, and is considered one of the greatest collegiate wrestlers in the history of the sport. He quickly became *the* best, but had to be patient in becoming *his* best.

So there's the contradiction. You must develop a sense of patience when it comes to reaching your potential, but at the same time, you must expect to be successful today. I've found that the key to establishing patience in my life has been to live without guilt. What I mean by that is, if I've done my very best in every aspect of my motivated life each and every day, then I can rest easy at night, knowing that I've given myself every possible chance to be successful. If, at the end of the day, I'm forced to wait a little longer until my dreams come true, that's okay. I will simply go to sleep tonight expecting to be successful tomorrow. You can lie to others about whether or not you've done your best, but you cannot lie to yourself. You either did your best or you didn't. You can't always control the outcome, but you *can* control your effort, and you can certainly be assured that you're taking the necessary actions to reach your goals.

Success Strategies

- By working to your capacity today and delaying the reward until later, you will receive a much greater end result.
- There truly is joy in the journey of success.
- You can't always control the outcome, but you can always control your effort.
- Expect immediate success, but be patient if it doesn't happen immediately.

When you're doing everything that you can possibly do, you too will have a patient, guilt-free life. You'll know that, while you may need to wait for your dreams to come true, your expectations and persistence will eventually get you where you want to go! But before you can live guilt-free, you must first learn to apply the lessons from the example of....

The Motivated Worker

Let me ask you a question. What do you think differentiates a person who makes $30,000 per year from a person who makes $250,000 per year? Most of time, when asked this question, people throw out answers like "education," "intelligence," or "hard work." While these may all be true on one level or another, let me steer your focus toward another answer.

When we focus exclusively on money, it's easy to overlook the fact that many people make salaries that would never classify them as rich, yet who love what they do and wouldn't change it for the world. These people are motivated in different areas than money. This example doesn't necessarily pertain to that group. Nonetheless, let me tell you that the most basic starting point in the differences between people who achieve these two different salaries is their *beliefs*. People who believe that they are worth more will inevitably find a way to make more. They don't believe that they're better than other people; they simply see themselves as a worthy investment.

Now let's move on to the main premise of my example. In addition to believing that they are worth the higher salary, people making a $250,000 salary actually had to apply for the job. That's right—just because they believed that they were worth it didn't mean that they were automatically going to make $250,000. They still had to go out and apply.

How many of you know someone—or maybe you *are* someone—who is constantly complaining about how much they make, or how broke they are; yet they never do anything to make a change in their lives? I have a friend who constantly complains about his job. He says that he works incredibly hard and makes almost no money. He can't pay off his credit card because he has no cash flow. He can't go out with all of his friends on the weekends and do the things he wants to do. Most of the time, he's simply complaining and not really looking to make things better. However, one day he said to me, "I'm thinking of looking for a new job. Will you help me?"

"Absolutely!" I said. My first question for him was, "So, what do you want to do?"

He said, "I don't really care. I'd just like to change my lifestyle and make more money. I don't really like what I'm doing right now, so anything's got to be better."

So my next question was, "How much money would you like to make in the next year?" He said that he would love to make $100,000. This was a big jump, as he was currently making $39,000, but in my opinion, it wasn't too far-fetched. He had a college degree, was extremely intelligent, and had great people skills. My next question to him was, "Do you really believe that you're worth that much money?"

He quickly responded, "Sure." So, naturally, I next suggested he peruse the classified sections in three of our local papers for ads that met his criteria. After he had picked out which jobs he wanted to apply for, my wife and I were to talk with him more about his resume and prepare him for potential interview questions and strategies.

A few weeks went by before I happened to see him again. "You're going to be so proud of me," he said. "I just started the process of applying for one of the jobs we spoke about."

"Okay, which job was that?"

Bursting with excitement, he said, "I applied for that job where a friend of mine works."

Knowing the place he was speaking of, I immediately asked, "For which position in the company?" He replied that he'd applied for basically the same type of job that he was currently doing.

Now, you already know my next question. It is the only logical question that comes to mind at this point, especially when you know that he disliked his job function and that his main goal was to make more money. So here it comes…"How much does the position pay?"

His response? "$40,000."

Now, this whole scenario really amazed me. Why would someone state exactly what they wanted, and then fail to do everything to make it happen? Why would you set a huge goal, and then settle for something that's nowhere even close to the goal that you had already set? My goal here is to motivate you to reach for the stars, and once you reach upward for them, to *hold on* as tightly as you can until you've pulled yourself up to them! Now, if my friend had made a switch to do something that he thought was more rewarding, I wouldn't have been disappointed. If he was happy with where he was currently working and didn't want to change, I wouldn't have been disappointed. However, neither of these were the case. He was very clear that $100,000 was what he wanted, but he never threw his hat in the ring to give himself a chance of reaching his dreams.

Plain and simple, you have to apply! You have to apply for the job you want. You have to apply for the dreams that you want. You have to apply yourself! You are much better than you give yourself credit for being. You're much more capable than you're dreaming of being right now. A huge difference between the person who makes $30,000 and the person who makes $250,000 is the application.

What I want you to do today is write down your goals. Put them in a place where you'll see them constantly. Look at them daily, and don't negotiate the goals. Life will throw you curves. There will be times when you think that you can't or won't achieve those goals you've written down. And if you never reach that challenging time, then the goals that you've written down are not big enough. If you're truly reaching for the stars, you'll inevitably come up against a point in the journey when your dreams will seem too far-fetched. Don't give up! There are absolutely no limits to what you're capable of achieving.

Limits are like fears. They are all just illusions. —Michael Jordan

Success Strategies

- Only those who apply for what they want will ever be successful.

- Reach for the stars. Once you've reached upward for them, hold on as tightly as possible until you've pulled yourself up to them.

- Change your strategies if necessary, but never negotiate your goals.

- If your goals don't force you out of your comfort zone, then you're not dreaming big enough.

- There are absolutely no limits to what you are capable of achieving.

Chapter 11

THE ATTITUDE OF SUCCESS

Throughout my entire life, I've constantly looked to people ahead of me in every field and worked to reproduce their successes in my own life. Whether I'm learning from a gifted athlete at a sports camp, learning from an experienced teacher, listening to how-to audio books by high achievers, attending coaching programs by people who know my particular business, or even reading a book that was written to take me to higher levels of success, I've paid attention to successful models.

However, as I've gone through these different learning experiences, I've realized that other people interpret these classes or coaching sessions very differently from me. I've found that people have basically one of two different reactions when they look at someone else who is doing something spectacular. Most people will think, "That could never be me," or "They're so lucky!" This group sees success as unachievable, or only available to other people. Instead of looking at the possibilities that lie within themselves, they see only the deficiencies and personal inadequacies that will keep them from achieving the same success as those who are already at the top. These people either quickly dismiss the information being taught and choose to remain unchanged, or equally as depressing, talk about their inability to achieve the same results themselves, therefore bringing others down with them.

Don't be like them. Instead, there's a simple question to ask yourself when you're faced with trying times....

Why Not Me?

Psychologists have written for years about the importance of asking yourself questions. The most important thing is that you ask yourself the *right* questions. People who imagine success is unattainable most often look at every negative aspect of an event or circumstance, and will only focus on what is bad or unfair. When attempting to reproduce someone else's success in their own lives, they'll focus on their inabilities and personal deficiencies. The question that they begin to ask themselves is, "Why me?" They think they have bad luck. They feel like the whole world is raining on their parade. They feel like success in any endeavor is some unattainable commodity only enjoyed by those people born with some kind of a "gift." And I have found that most people who think this way in one area of their lives will typically expand that same negativity into every other aspect of their lives as well. Unfortunately, this group of people makes up 95 percent of the population.

As for the second group, they are the ones who believe that they can reproduce the success of another person. This group is filled with success and endless possibilities. The people in this group learn from and implement the strategies of more successful people and believe that "what one man can do, another can do." This group will consistently be the highest achievers in all that they do, and will be living a motivated life. This second group—which is only, 5 percent of the population, remember—is the one that I want you to be a part of as you begin to implement the practical applications of this book. Getting you from group one to group two is one of my goals for you as you read this book. Once you learn to make a few subtle changes in your thoughts, you'll start to do what the successfully motivated do, and you too will begin to enjoy the motivated life that is waiting for you on the other side.

The great news is, if you're in the "why me?" group, it's very easy to move to the second group. You've only got to change your focus, then add a single word to the question you're asking yourself.

To start with the focus part of the equation, let's begin by making a simple switch to focusing on the possibilities rather than the problems.

We are surrounded by unlimited opportunities disguised as problems.
—John Maxwell

With the recent resurgence of books and programs like *The Secret*, we're once again being made aware of the wonderful benefits of focusing on what we want in order to achieve or acquire it. The various teachers involved in these programs are reiterating what has been taught by some of the most successful people the world has ever known. They are teaching about the power of *positive thinking*. From a practical standpoint, I want you to begin to look at the best possible outcome of every situation. That's right—the *best* possible outcome in every situation. Rather than focusing on what might go wrong, or how you cannot possibly do something, begin evaluating every situation by looking at what the best possible outcome would be. You'll find that you get what you focus on.

I remember, as you may as well, taking a driver's education course in high school. In learning the rules of the road, I was taught what to do when passing an oncoming car that has its bright lights on. You're supposed to focus on the outside line on the right side of the road. Looking straight ahead or at the oncoming car can potentially lead to collisions. However, simply by looking at the outside line, your car will begin to drift in that direction, cutting down your chances of being blinded by the light and ending up in an accident. In life, just as in your vehicle, you will go where you look.

As you are now aware, in addition to thinking and saying what you want, it is what you *do* with those thoughts and those words that matters most when it comes to living a motivated life. The next thing to do after focusing on the best possible outcome is to ask yourself the right question.

Instead of looking at the negatives or the roadblocks involved and thinking, "Why me?" you're going to begin looking at the best possible outcome and ask yourself, "Why *not* me?"

Asking myself this one simple question has put me in the proper mindset to accomplish my dreams as much as anything else that I've done. In sports, I remember thinking, "Someone's going to be a state champion... why not me?" In school, I remember thinking, "Someone's going to earn an A in this class... why not me?" In business, I remember thinking, "Someone's going to run a successful clinic... why not me?" Get the point? Focus on the best outcome, then ask yourself, "Why not me?" As you already know, you *are* worth it. You deserve success. You were made for greatness.

If living a motivated life in every aspect is available to everyone, and that life would be the best possible outcome of reading this book, then ask yourself the question, "Why not me?" I will guarantee you that someone right now is living at a level that you could reach if you applied yourself. I'll guarantee you that someone else will read this book and implement these strategies en route to living a motivated life. The question is, will you? If someone will both get and give everything possible to this life, why shouldn't that person be you?

Even if you've been in a repetitive cycle of negative thinking and have believed that you cannot possibly *be, do,* and *have* certain things in life, realize that you have a choice.

In an interview with Robert Downey Jr., Oprah asked him about how his life had spun out of control into a world of drug addiction. Here he was, on top of the world as a highly sought-after actor who had conquered one role after another with endless praise. He responded by saying that he'd been wrapped up in negative thinking, and continued to let himself be controlled by something that was very easy to quit. Oprah quickly responded, "Wait. You mean to tell me that you, Robert Downey Jr., think that it is easy to stop using drugs?"

He responded, "Absolutely. It is the *decision* to quit that is the hard part. Quitting is very easy."[3]

> *You cannot change your destination overnight,*
> *but you can change your direction overnight.* —Jim Rohn

Success Strategies

- You go where you look.
- Imagine the best possible outcome and ask yourself, "Why not me?"
- If someone is going to be successful, why shouldn't that someone be you?
- Stop focusing on problems and start focusing on solutions.
- Changing your life is easy. The decision to change is the hard part.

So again, even if you've led a life without incorporating a "why not me?" attitude, make the decision to implement it today. And while you're asking yourself "why not me?" I'll pose the following question to you myself....

What if You Had To?

When you are motivated for life, you treat everything you do as a "have to." You "have to" be your best in sports. You "have to" be your best at work. You "have to" be your best at home. Motivated people understand that they "have to" be their best *today*. As Walter Payton said, "Tomorrow is promised to no one." Those who go through life waiting to do the things that they *can* do, *should* do, and *need* to do, will come to the end of their lives saying the worst phrases possible:

---

3   Robert Downey Jr., interviewed by Oprah Winfrey, *The Oprah Winfrey Show*, November 23, 2004.

- "I could have."

- "I would have."

- "I should have."

My mother often repeated an example given to her once by her pastor. He said that he saw life as a test. And just as in the tests you took in school, such as the SAT and the ACT, the time will one day come when God says, "Okay, time's up. Turn in your test." Where you stand at that point is how you finish. What you have done at that point is all that you'll ever do. This lesson is one that she recalls often, reminding her that we need to grasp the opportunities in front of us today. We never know when our time will be up.

Grasp the opportunities that lie in front of you right now. Go at those opportunities with a "have to" mindset. Go after your *be*, *do*, and *have* goals like your life depends on it. While you may not physically die if you don't achieve your full potential, you'll never truly live a motivated life. So in a way, your life, at least the motivated life that you could have, does depend on doing what's necessary today. My best recommendation for you is to go after your dreams with a "have to" mindset *before* you actually "have to." Being proactive is the easiest, most efficient way to achieve your dreams. And you can do more right now than you give yourself credit for.

One of my chiropractor colleagues is a perfect example of what you're capable of when you "have to." After several years as a solo practitioner, he decided to take on an additional physician in his office to lighten his load, as well as to take his clinic to the next level. He began to look for associates, but continually ran into problems and came up with excuses for why he couldn't find the help he needed. Three months went by, and he had no success in getting help. Six months went by with the same excuses. Nine months later, he still had not found a single person who could help him out. A full year after he had begun his search for an associate, he was no closer to finding a good worker to help him achieve his mission of helping more people. As he tells the story, he says that he had used every excuse possible for why he was unable to find good help:

- "There are just no doctors available."
- "All of the good doctors are already taken."
- "There's no one available in my state."
- "No one is interested in becoming an associate."

One Saturday afternoon about a year after beginning his search, he was making some home improvements. Noticing that some shingles needed to be fixed, he climbed up on the roof. While he was working, he slipped and fell off of the roof onto his elbows, fracturing both arms in multiple places. As a chiropractor, your arms are essential to providing your services to your patients. Knowing that he would be unable to physically treat his patients himself, he was faced that Saturday afternoon with the choice of closing his office down or employing another physician to take his place. Remember that, at this point, he'd been looking for an associate for well over a year with no success. But only two days after the fall, he managed to place an associate in his office with a contract signed on Monday. Up until that point, he had not approached his goal with a "have to" mindset. In contrast, when faced with a problem in which his practice and financial life depended upon his ability to find an immediate solution, he found a qualified and competent associate with ease. What is interesting to me is that the only circumstance that changed after his fall was that he *did* what he knew he should have done before the fall. He had ideas already about how he could find the help he needed, but only after he was faced with an immediate dilemma did he take the action he knew was necessary.

Not only did he use this experience to take him to higher levels of success, but he is now also a chiropractic coach who is unable to accept excuses from his clients. He knows what you are truly capable of if you approach a situation with a "have to" mindset.

I believe that the lesson here is that we are capable of more right now than we give ourselves credit for. The key is to adopt a "have to" mindset without first falling off the roof! Don't wait for the bottom to drop out before you go after what you want. Financial experts say that every person should have a six-month emergency fund in case the worst happens. With a little bit of concentrated action, everyone could make the changes necessary to save some extra money so that their emergency fund is ready. Instead, when things are good, most Americans forget about saving money in a six-month contingency account. Ask anyone you know, and they will all agree that this would be a very easy, safe way to approach their financial future, yet very few people actually do it. *Do* what you know you should do now, before the worst happens. Approach your goals proactively with a "have to," mindset and you'll be amazed at how the so-called "worst" never happens. Bumps in the road are minor because you are prepared for them through being proactive in *doing* what you know to do.

After the 2008 Olympics, champion Michael Phelps was asked what he thought about at the beginning of the race. What do you think his one thought was as he set Olympic and world swimming records in multiple events? His response was, "I can't lose!" Now *that* is a "have to" mindset!

You'll find all top, motivated achievers approach the tasks in front of them with a "must win" or "can't lose" mindset. If you want to achieve a motivated life, use this same approach to help you excel and do the things necessary to succeed today.

In Tim Ferris's book *The 4-Hour Work Week*, he discusses this principle as he explains the thinking necessary to go from a forty-hour workweek to a four-hour workweek. He poses the following questions:

> *If you had a heart attack and had to work two hours per day, what would you do? The doctor has warned you, after triple bypass surgery, that if you don't cut down your work to two hours per day for the first three months post-op, you will die. How would you do it? ... If you had a second heart attack and had to work two hours per week, what would you do? ... If you had a gun to your head and*

had to stop doing 4/5 of different time-consuming activities, what would you remove?[4]

If your life depended on it, I'll guarantee that you could find a way to make these things happen. And if we know that it is possible, why not go for it now? You're capable of doing amazing things when you decide that you *have* to do them. Everyone has heard the unbelievable stories of hundred-pound women who inexplicably lifted thousand-pound vehicles to save their children pinned beneath them. How does this happen? They see no obstacles in front of them when saving their children's lives—only solutions. The car needs to be lifted so that the child can live. Period. They don't have time to analyze their own weight versus the weight of the vehicle, or to come up with a million excuses about why they can't do it. They just decide what needs to be done, and then they do what they need to do to make it happen.

Before we go forward, let's revisit your goals. If success was your only option and failure was not a possibility, what would you do? Are your goals big enough? Are your dreams worthy of what you truly have to offer? If we're going to go after these goals as if our lives depended on it, let's shoot for the moon! The following quote is one of my all-time favorites. I read it to myself each morning and also have it printed on a card in my wallet so that I can review it throughout my day:

As God's chosen, blessed sons and daughters, we are expected to attempt something large enough that failure is guaranteed... unless God steps in.
—Bruce Wilkinson

So if you revisit your goals and they now appear too easy, now is the time to update them and to grow your vision. Remember, you will not fail! You are going after these goals as if you have no choice but to accomplish them. Dream bigger! Remember, as Les Brown said, "Shoot for the moon. Even if you fall short, you still end up being a star."

In the art of war, Sun Tzu said that if you want to get the most out of your army, "once your soldiers have climbed the gates, burn the ladders."

---

4   Timothy Ferriss, *The 4-Hour Workweek*, 78.

Obviously, if this were to happen, the only way for the soldiers to leave is to fight their way to victory. If the same were true for you and your current dreams and challenges, could you do it? If you *had* to make your dreams a reality in order to move forward in life, could you? I'll guarantee that you could make it happen. In fact, if you implement the ideas and procedures in this book, I'll guarantee that you *will* make it happen.

According to Anthony Galie, author of *Take Control of your Subconscious Mind*, one key in this process is to remember that you always have a choice.[5] You don't really have to do anything. There may be consequences to your actions, but you can choose to do or *not* to do anything. You don't really have to work. Now, there may be consequences and financial difficulties to follow, but you don't have to go. You don't have to eat right and stay healthy. You may develop premature health difficulties and risk dying early, but you still do not have to eat healthy. I find this to be a liberating thought. I don't have to do anything that I don't want to do. Essentially, it has been this way our entire lives. We have, and have always had, a choice in everything that we do or *don't* do. If we thought that we *needed* to do something, we were just kidding ourselves. We convinced ourselves that we had to. My point is that you already know how to convince yourself that you "have to" do things; you convince yourself *all the time*. So here are what I believe to be the most important actions to take in order to hold yourself accountable and go after your goals with a "have to" mindset:

- Find your purpose.
- Plan your dreams and goals.
- Write down your dreams and goals.
- Visualize your goals and dreams (along with the feeling you will have when you accomplish or acquire them).
- Read books about others that have accomplished similar goals and dreams.

---

5   Anthony Galie, Take Control of Your Subconscious Mind.

- Listen to audios and watch videos about people who have accomplished similar goals and dreams.

- Seek out and talk to people who have done the things that you want to do.

- Take pictures of your dreams.

- Review your goals and dreams daily.

- Speak your goals and dreams to others who can help to hold you accountable.

- Find a coach or mentor who will help you hold yourself accountable.

Do the things necessary to make your dreams come true by going after your dreams and goals with a "have to" mindset!

Chapter 12

CREATING ACCOUNTABILITY

It's essential for you to speak your goals out loud to yourself and to others if you plan to make them happen. When I was a fourteen-year-old kid in the eighth grade, I attended a wrestling camp coached by a former Olympian. One night, he and I were talking after a session, and he asked me what my goal was for high school wrestling. I told him that I believed that I could be a four-time state champion, winning as a high school freshman, sophomore, junior, and senior. This was a lofty goal, since I'd never competed in a single high school event, not to mention that I was divulging this goal to a former Olympian. The following day, the entire camp of several hundred other athletes, in which I was one of the youngest campers, was brought together for a closing inspirational talk. After getting everyone fired up, the coach asked me to stand up in front of the entire group. He said, "This is Mike Mason. Mike is in the eighth grade and will compete in high school next year. Mike, please tell the group what you plan to accomplish. What is your dream?"

There was no backing out at this point. I stood there in front of several hundred wrestlers, many of which I would be competing against, and said, "My goal is to be a four-time state champion."

Had he not placed me in that position of having to speak my dream, I never would have made that statement. Nonetheless, here I was, having spoken my commitment to my dreams in front of hundreds of people. At that point, I felt like I "had to" do everything in my power to live up to my words. I went on to earn a record of 112–1, becoming a three-time state champion, with my only high school loss coming my freshman year in the state finals. Although I fell short of my goal of being a four-time state champion, I did everything in my power to make my dream a reality because I had committed myself to it in front of my peers.

Speaking Your Dreams

Speaking your dream is a powerful way to hold yourself accountable for doing the things necessary to accomplish your dreams. I've always used peer pressure to my advantage by speaking my dream to others. Begin believing in and following the rule that you must always do what you *say* you will do. You'll be able to approach your goals with a "have to" mindset. I tell the relevant people in my life about my goals. I speak my business goals to my staff. I speak my family goals to my wife and parents. I speak my personal goals to my wife. I've even hired my own coaches, to who I divulge my goals and dreams so that they can also help me to hold myself accountable.

As a central example, when I had the vision of creating Unstoppable Success, I immediately went home and told my wife my plans. I then called my best friend and told him about my plans. I continued to tell everyone who would listen what I planned to create with this dream and the purpose behind it. Having told so many people, I then had no choice but to follow through. I used peer pressure to help me gain the "have to" mindset that I knew I would need to make the dream a reality.

Need additional motivation to make your dreams happen? Remember that if you have established a purpose that is centered on others, then you "have to" accomplish your dreams and goals for *them*. You always have a choice, so choose to go after your dreams as if your life, and the lives of your friends and family members, depended on your success. Don't get overwhelmed; get excited! You can and will make it happen. Remind yourself daily that you always have a choice and that you are choosing to approach your goals with a "have to" mindset. And when your day is done, let it go. If you've truly done all that is within your power to do on a given day, then you can, as my coach always told me, "Weigh your results in peace, knowing that you did your best."

By the way, if you have faith in God, I should remind you that God is always watching and that he expects us to do what we are supposed to do and are capable of doing. This is the ultimate "have to" motivation. Don't forget it!

Success Strategies

- Go after your goals with a "Zen koan" mindset.
- All successful people approach their goals with a "must win" or "can't lose" attitude.
- You *always* have a choice. Choose to be successful.
- Use peer pressure to your advantage by speaking your goals to people who will hold you accountable.
- With a purpose centered on others, you *must* achieve your goals to benefit them.

Only when you are truly committed to speaking your goals and creating a "have to" attitude will you surround yourself with the essential people described in....

The Rule of Three

My father taught me at an early age the importance of what he called the "Rule of Three." I have used this rule in virtually every aspect of my life to help create and maintain a motivated attitude. The rule is that, in any area that you are committed to, you need to surround yourself with three different people. One of the people is ahead of you, one is behind you, and one is equal to you. There are no limits on how many people or groups you have in each of these three categories, but it's crucial that you have at least one person identified in each group.

The first task is finding someone ahead of you. In sports, this would be someone who has already achieved the success that you are looking to have in the future, or at least someone who has already been more successful than the level you're at currently. In other areas of life, such as parenting, it can be someone who's simply done a good job of properly developing their own children, as you would like to do. The key is to find someone in this area who is motivated to do their best and whom you would like to emulate. We'll discuss in a later chapter the importance of recognizing and following inspired and motivated people, but in short, this person must be someone whose footsteps you could imagine following. Do your research; if you settle for someone who's successful but doesn't have the kind of motivated life you're looking for, you won't gain much. If you haven't asked already, you'll be amazed at how forthcoming most successful people will be with their insights. I've repeatedly sought out such people in different areas of my life, and have never been denied an opportunity to meet with them and learn from them. In sports, I've always surrounded myself with at least one person who was better than me. I used the success of that person to motivate me until I'd reached their level. Once I'd caught up to them, I sought out better competition. I also consistently sought out additional coaches. I was very fortunate to have middle school and high school coaches who had very large knowledge bases and were willing to bring me up to their levels. At the same time, my coaches also knew that my own personal goals were beyond the level of success that they'd achieved themselves, so my coaches, my father, and I worked to find additional coaches who had achieved on an even larger scale. Amazingly, these people are not very hard to find. Even minimal effort will lead you to the person you need to help get you where you want to go. Again, let me remind you that the goal in finding these people to emulate is to become *your* best, not simply to compete against them. If necessary, revisit the chapter on competition.

Another key to this process is that you must remain coachable. Put your ego aside and learn from everything and anyone that can help you. One of my best friends and college teammate, Sam, is a perfect example of this. While we were in college, Sam and I consistently pushed each other to get better. We also both sought out the help of athletes who were more successful than we were. However, Sam did one thing that I did not. Sam also sought help from teammates who weren't as good as he was. Anytime he saw someone perform a technique that he wished to learn, he immediately approached them at the end of practice to learn from them. As for me, at the time I let my ego get in the way of asking someone younger or less successful for advice. In many areas, Sam improved much more quickly than me, because he was willing to learn from anyone. Since then, I've followed in his footsteps and tried to remember that I can learn something from anyone.

Please remember that no matter how good you become at anything, you need to remain coachable. Even professional athletes and owners of some of the largest, most successful businesses in the world still have coaches who can help them to remain focused and motivated.

In business, I always look for people who are achieving higher levels of success than me. I sometimes have to remove myself from my immediate surroundings so as to not appear competitive with the person who I'm hoping to emulate, but I've always found the right people to lead me to my goals. It has also been fun to find people who do not necessarily have larger businesses than mine, but who are more successful in one particular aspect than I am. You'll quickly find that everyone is better than you at something. If that something is an aspect in which you wish to improve, learn from them and apply it to your own life.

One intriguing and exciting aspect of this process is that, after reading the books of motivated people or being around motivated people long enough, I've found that I begin to ask myself what they would tell me to do. Essentially, I am coaching myself, based on what I believe they would tell me to do. For example, I spent so much time with one of my favorite coaches that I can still see him standing next to me when I'm running, saying, "Pick it up, pick it up, pick it up!" Over ten years after having him as a coach, I still use that image of him to motivate myself to do better.

As another example, after reading one of my favorite business books, I decided to join the author's seminar and coaching program for the following twelve months. Even though I had not yet met the author, simply reading her book allowed me to start asking myself the same questions that I believed she would ask me when I got there. I believed she'd ask me a simple question: "What would you do if you had to double your business?" Even before I attended the seminar, I decided that the answer would be to open a second clinic. I then applied the various principles in this book, along with the self-coaching procedures that I'd learned from other successful people, to open a second location before I had even met my new coach. And I did all of this because I could already see her asking me the question that would lead me to that answer. Simply by reading her book, I began to think like her, and was able to do what she wanted me to in order to get to the next level.

I cannot overstress the importance of this process. Whatever it is that you're trying to achieve, there will be someone available to help you if you are looking. By reading their books, listening to them speak, and spending time with them in any capacity, you'll begin to think like them, even when they're not around. And once you follow that up with doing what they do, you'll begin to experience the same success that they enjoy.

When the student is ready, the teacher will appear. —Buddhist proverb

Another thing that separates motivated people from everyone else is their ability to shoot for the moon. Don't look for someone mediocre to follow, but rather look for someone who's truly amazing at what they do. In every aspect of life in which I have looked for a leader to follow, I've gone straight to the top. In sports, I sought the help of former Olympians, world champions, and national champions. In finances, I sought the personal advice of multimillionaires. In business, I sought the help of the top instructors in the country. As a physician, I sought the help of the top physicians in the country. Especially with the Internet, these people are easy to find and much more readily available to you than you realize. Through meeting and "mini-interviewing" these people, I've gained more confidence in my own abilities by seeing that they are still ordinary people—ordinary people doing extraordinary things.

A truly motivated person will always have at least one person whom they look to for advice as they continue to grow in each area. And when looking for leadership, don't sell yourself short. Go straight to the top!

I not only use all of the brains that I have, but all that I can borrow.
—Woodrow Wilson

Your second task for the Rule of Three is to find a person who's behind you and bring them on the journey with you. I've often found this task to be the most rewarding and fun to be a part of. That said, it's difficult to announce that you are "ahead" of someone and would like to bring them along. Occasionally, the person will know that you're leading them without being told; they may even wish to be led by you. However, I've found that most people don't seek out leaders (in other words, they don't follow of the Rule of Three), but instead let the winds take them where they may. That's why it's important to identify at least one person to bring along with you. As you grow, feed them more information.

As an example, in athletics, I've often identified individuals with tremendous potential whom I believed would not only benefit from my experience and knowledge, but also would be interested in implementing my advice. As a student, I've often found study groups in which I could invite at least one person whom I knew could use the help—and once there, I made sure that they received it. In business, I've referred many new business owners to the books and coaches that have made me successful.

Again, it is not necessary to announce that you are bringing someone along with you. It's also not necessary to tell anyone else about the help you're giving them. Simply do it because it's the right thing to do. What I've found is that, by helping these people, I become even more motivated to remain ahead of them in that area so that I can continue to help them. If and when they catch up to my level, I will push them to follow someone better than me. This is where you must once again look at your purpose in being motivated for life. If your emphasis is on reaching your own potential so that you can help others reach theirs, you'll never run out of energy, and you'll never lose your motivation to be your best!

What sorts of things can you do to help people reach their potential?

- Send them your favorite book.
- Send them your favorite quotes.
- Give them frequent encouragement.
- Refer them to your favorite teachers or coaches.
- Refer them to your favorite seminars or audio programs.
- Give them insights into what has made you successful.

Your third task for the Rule of Three is to find a person whom you consider your equivalent. This person is also a crucial part of the process. For those who enjoy healthy competition, this person is must. This person is often with whom you'll bounce ideas back and forth. The goal in identifying this person is to allow you to measure your progress. As you continue to grow in the area that you have in common with this person, they will provide an excellent gauge on your improvement. I've found that I not only receive excellent feedback on my own ideas from these people, but also, as with the previous group we discussed, I find joy and energy in their success.

Being motivated for life requires you to know when to lead, and when to be led. Identifying three people in each area that you wish to improve will allow you to do so. Identify these people and begin utilizing these resources—as well as becoming the resource—today!

Never miss an opportunity to teach and never miss
an opportunity to learn. —Mike Mason

Success Strategies

- Find someone ahead of you to follow, someone behind you to lead, and someone equal to you to compete with.

- Know when to lead and when to be led.

- You can learn from everyone, since everyone is better than you at something. Remain coachable.

- Choose your leaders carefully and only follow the best of the best.

- Only when you reach your own potential can you help others reach theirs.

Just remember that the goal is not simply to identify someone in each of the three categories, but rather to identify the *right* person in each of the categories. And in order to find the right person, you must master the art of....

Recognizing Greatness

If there's one thing that I feel is essential to being motivated for life, it is the ability to recognize greatness. As the Rule of Three shows, you'll need to look to others for help, as well as take others with you on your way. If you do not have a good grasp of this concept, the advice you get from those seemingly ahead of you will lead you astray, and those you're leading will pull you down. You must become astute at developing instincts and learning to recognize greatness in others. If you want to be exceptional at anything yourself, you need to surround yourself with other exceptional people. However, if you don't learn to recognize greatness, you'll inevitably find yourself surrounded by mediocrity, and as you now know, that's not good enough!

As you continue your journey toward a motivated life, you'll find it easier to distinguish the great from the ordinary. You will find that motivated people in any endeavor act a certain way and talk a certain way. They're honest people who are driven to get better at everything that they do. However, as former president Ronald Reagan declared, "Trust but verify!" You need to trust your instincts, but always check with others that your assumptions are correct.

As an athlete, I not only wanted to emulate successful athletes in my sport, but I also wanted to follow those who placed importance on the same values as me. While I feel that I've always had a knack for being drawn toward the great instructors at sports camps, this became most apparent to me as I entered college. Having met with several potential coaches from various universities, I feel that I could have learned a lot from every one of them. But when I met Coach Nate Carr, I knew that he was the one for me to follow. His athletic credentials were incredible, but so were a lot of the coaches'. It was the way he spoke, the goals he had for the program and his athletes, and the confidence he displayed in his ability to get others where they wanted to go. Having struggled with the decision for several months, I made up my mind the second I met Nate. I knew that he was a person with the kind of integrity, motivation, and energy that would bring out the best in me.

As a coach, I've always tried to do the same as Nate. Coaches need to be able to look at athletes and see not only where they are currently, but where they could be if given the right opportunity and instruction. The best coaches in any sport are the ones who can assemble the best teams from the start. Once you have the right people in the right positions, then you can coach them to success. This is a gamble that all professional coaches take when they spend extreme amounts of money to bring in potential superstars. The most successful coaches have developed their instincts for recognizing greatness. How many times have you seen a player dropped from a professional sports team, only to be snatched right up by another team? The other coach has detected potential greatness in that player. Many times, you'll see the world's greatest athletes go through this process, in which a coach has taken special interest in them because of something that shows their potential. More often than not, what those coaches see is an attitude. Physical attributes are extremely important, especially as you move up the ladder of competition, but coaches know that athletes who are motivated and determined to be their best are more likely to make it than "gifted" athletes who lack motivation.

Success is largely a part of hanging on after others have let go.
—William Feather

Growing up in sports, I was constantly surrounded by other athletes and multiple coaches. Even in sports in which I did not participate, I saw that athletes who were most successful shared an attitude of endless motivation. I became so focused on duplicating the successes of these people that I eventually developed the same motivated attitude as them. Once I had it, it became much easier to see those with it, as well as those trying to get it.

As a coach at various sports camps, including my own, I've found myself among thousands of athletes every summer—but only a few stand out. In those camps, there are two people in particular who always come to mind when I think about recognizing greatness. The first person came to a camp that I was holding at my high school. At the end of every camp, I hold my version of the "iron man" competition. I divide the camp into two age groups, with the younger kids in the morning (ages 5–10) and the older kids in the afternoon (ages 11–18). The kids perform multiple physical exercises, basically to the point of exhaustion. The young athletes can quit the competition anytime that they choose, and we have cold water waiting for them immediately. We continue until three people are left standing, at which point we go to the pull-up bar. Each person is then placed on the pull-up bar, where they are to simply grip the bar and hold themselves up without touching the ground or the wall. The last one left hanging is the winner.

One year, during a morning session of our iron man competition, an eight-year-old named Brandon won the competition and was the last one hanging onto the bar. Following his early morning win, he decided that he wanted to compete with the afternoon group as well. Keep in mind that Brandon was only eight years old, and many of the afternoon campers were twice his age and weighed over a hundred pounds more. Further, several of the afternoon campers were returning high school state champions. As the competition played out, young Brandon found his way into the final three. He was nine years younger than the other two competitors. As the two older athletes reached up to grasp the pull-up bar, with all of the other campers cheering as they looked on, I had to pick up young Brandon, who was unable to reach the bar by himself. About a minute into hanging, the two older boys began to grunt and moan. One of the participants was even crying, not wanting to give up and lose the competition. As I looked at Brandon, he stared straight ahead while his little arms quivered, not showing one ounce of emotion. As time progressed, one high school athlete dropped, and then the other, leaving only Brandon hanging in the end. When I helped him down, the unwavering look in his eyes told me that he'd known he was going to be the last one on that bar.

I called my college coach the following day and told him to keep an eye out for Brandon in the future. When he asked how old he was and I responded "eight," he had a nice chuckle. I proceeded to tell him that this was the most mentally tough kid that I'd ever been around, and that I knew he would be successful one day. Years later, Brandon was everything that I knew he could be. He was a four-time high school state champion and was one of the most highly touted athletes in the country. He is already a two-time NCAA All-American and is working toward becoming an NCAA champion. The important part to remember is my recognition of his potential had *nothing* to do with his wrestling technique. I recognized his greatness in the attitude and determination that he possessed, even as an eight-year-old.

The other athlete who serves as a perfect example of this concept was in the eighth grade when I met him. Once again, I was an instructor at a wrestling camp when I was introduced to this young man. Unfortunately, he had broken his arm the week prior to the camp, and sported a full cast for the entire week. As I was teaching technique, I noticed his look of determination and frustration as he stood on the sidelines and watched. At the end of practice, I noticed him performing every conditioning exercise that he could with one arm. Most athletes use an injury as an excuse to sit out of the conditioning, but this young man let nothing stand in the way of joining in. Following the conditioning that evening, I went out to eat with some of the other coaches before returning to the hotel. When I arrived, I happened to notice that this same kid was also coming back to the hotel with headphones on, dripping with sweat. He'd been out for a run. As I approached him, I commented, "I'm going to have to do a better job at running the conditioning tomorrow if you still have leftover energy today."

As he wiped the sweat from his forehead, he replied, "You never know when there's not going to be a tomorrow." I was impressed, and I quickly got his name so that I could track his future and reported his name back to my college coach. A few years later, I was unsurprised to learn that he had also gone on to win four high school state titles and was also one of the top recruits in the country. Please remember, I recognized his potential without having ever seen him perform. His attitude was a telltale sign of where he was going.

In business, I've found this concept to be essential, but also an ongoing challenge. As with coaching, the goal is to establish the best team possible. In order to do this, you must be able to recognize greatness in the hiring processes. Potential employees are going to put their best foot forward for their interview, so you must become adept at determining which people are motivated and which ones are not. Recognizing motivated people and choosing to establish a team that consists solely of motivated members is one of the most important aspects of the hiring process. If people have not shown me that they can be motivated in other aspects of their lives, then I wait until better candidates come along. Again, I do not claim to have mastered this skill, but I do recognize its importance.

It starts when I am reviewing resumes and references. As I mentioned earlier in the book, several of the people whom I've interviewed for my businesses have recommendation letters that were written over ten years ago, even though they have worked in other positions much more recently. I am not interested in what they did ten years ago; I'm interested in whether or not they are currently living a motivated life. I like to ask questions that will reveal the person's drive. I am not nearly as concerned about ability as I am about motivation and potential. If someone is determined to be successful, their abilities will soon follow.

If you're currently an employee, think about this for a moment. Do you work with people who are unmotivated? Do you have coworkers who show up to work just to put in their time so that they can get a paycheck? Do you have coworkers who enter the office in a bad mood, hating every second of their work? Do you have coworkers who complain excessively about management and how little they care about their employer, manager, and job? I'll bet at least one person comes to mind. How does it make you feel to be around that person? Not very good! Suddenly, your day seems even worse. You begin to lose motivation to do your best as well, don't you?

So, a few suggestions for you: If you are this person whom I just described, it stops this second. You need to realize, as we have already discussed, that you always have a choice. You can choose to be happy. You can choose to be motivated. You can choose to enjoy your job. You can even choose to quit your job and get a new one. Regardless, take immediate action and step it up today!

If your coworkers behave this way, choose to stop spending time with them, at least at work. They deserve no additional attention. Don't let someone else bring you down! Instead, choose to bring them up. As you know, this is not an easy task, but it is one that will prove advantageous for everyone in the group when you are successful. Take other people's lack of motivation as a chance to shine even brighter and exude a motivated attitude. As an employer, I immediately reward the most motivated people and let everyone else know about it. If less motivated coworkers do not feel challenged enough by this to step up their game, I begin looking for new, motivated team members to replace them.

This principle of recognizing greatness can be applied in finding the right friends, the right employer, the right doctor, and so on. However, in my opinion, the two aspects of your life in which it's most important to recognize greatness is in choosing a spouse and choosing a leader. Choosing a spouse or partner is a complete book in and of itself. The only thing that I will direct you toward noticing is that most of the top achievers and leaders in the world have indicated that choosing your spouse or partner is the most important decision you will ever make in your lifetime. So if your future relies so much on your decision, then you'd better be able to recognize potential greatness in other people. If you don't, your future will not be nearly as productive and enjoyable. However, when you choose the right person, the sky's the limit for both of you.

That said, let's focus on recognizing greatness in a leader. As you learned from the Rule of Three, selecting the right people to follow is equally as important as, if not more important than, any other aspect of getting motivated in any aspect of life. One of the first things to realize is that most people who dispense advice are not actually *doing* what they suggest. They are the "do as I say, not as I do" people of the world. So, the first rule in finding people to emulate is to trust what they say, but verify that their actions match their words. I've found that, with even minimal research or simply by asking around, you'll be able to get a pretty good grasp of a person's track record. I obviously want to follow other motivated people, but I also want to be certain their achievements are ethical and honest. Any potential leader whose values appear contrary to mine is immediately discarded from my list of influencers. This doesn't necessarily mean that I won't take advice from them, but I certainly take it with a grain of salt. Please make sure that you understand this point. It's extremely easy to be led astray. We are constantly looking for people to follow, whether we do it consciously or subconsciously, and typically, we're looking to improve the most important parts of our lives. Don't ever put your future in the hands of the wrong person. Don't ever put your family's future in the hands of the wrong person. Don't ever put your business in the hands of the wrong person. Don't ever put your finances in the hands of the wrong person. Look for greatness in anyone that you'll potentially follow, especially when it comes to these key aspects. Ask yourself whether they have bright futures of their own as well. Only take marital advice from those who have great marriages. Take business advice only from those who have their own successful businesses. Take financial advice only from those who are financially secure themselves, and not merely looking to make money by advising you. This is your life. Hopefully, by now you're starting to understand the importance of being able to recognize greatness in others, especially in leadership positions.

As I have already mentioned, while playing sports I gravitated toward a coach whose athletic and personal background backed up my own instincts about what a great person and motivator he appeared to be. While in school, I looked for the most clinically sound practitioners to learn about diagnosis and treatment. However, most of the time, those people were not very business savvy. So, I worked to find other people who had successful businesses of their own for business leadership. Sometimes, leaders that I choose to follow in one area may be lacking in another. I simply learn from their areas of strength and choose other leaders for other aspects. I want to be motivated to give my best and get everything I can from every aspect of life. This means that I need several coaches, not just one. But in all of them, I *first* have to recognize their greatness, then simply follow their examples.

For example, I once joined a nationally known financial education program. The program consisted of various instruction materials, introductions to future "connections," personal coaching calls, and three seminars throughout the year. After receiving the educational books and audios prior to the first meeting, I was so enthused that I shut nearly everything else down for two days so that I could immerse myself in the material. By the time I got to the first seminar, I'd gone through all of the materials several times. Most seminars are taught by businessmen and businesswomen who have successfully completed the courses and been trained by the company owner. But for at least an hour or two each day, the company owner came to teach herself.

Eagerly anticipating her arrival, I watched as she entered the back of our instruction facility. For nearly thirty minutes, I watched her as she intensely scoured the room, as the various attendees from different businesses and backgrounds asked and answered questions from the current instructor. Not yet understanding the situation, I continued to follow her every move and gesture until her presentation began. While the information in her session was useful, I couldn't help but wonder about her purpose in evaluating the room from the back of the class before being introduced. Immediately after her class, her reasoning became much more apparent. She quickly approached a few different people in the room and addressed each one of them by their first name, as if she had known them for years. Then, she proceeded to tell each person about different business opportunities that she had for each of them, tailored to their current occupations. What has made her exceptional is her ability to recognize greatness in others. Once she recognizes other great people, she forms strategic business alliances with them to propel her businesses forward with *their* skills. The majority of her empire has been built using the strengths and talents of other people, with her as the facilitator and overseer of the larger plan. To this day, she is one of the most successful people whom I have had the pleasure to meet—and remember; her greatest strength is her ability to recognize greatness in others. It's just as important to master this concept for a leader as for a follower.

Success Strategies

- Trust others, but verify what you learn from them.
- Surround yourself with those who have strengths in your areas of weakness.
- Successful people outlast everyone else.
- Successful people can distinguish the good from the great.
- Choosing a leader and choosing a spouse are two of the biggest decisions you will ever make. Choose them wisely.

In mastering this concept, you will learn that the two most important words in your life will be….

Chapter 13

BECOMING UNSTOPPABLE

Becoming Unstoppable

The winners in life think constantly in terms of I can,
I will and I am. Losers, on the other hand, concentrate t
heir waking thoughts on what they should have or would
have done, or what they can't do. —Dennis Waitley

According to the legendary Milt Campbell, former Olympic gold medalist in the decathlon, the most important words in the pursuit of success are the words "I am." As a high school athlete, he began to tell himself, "I am the greatest athlete in the world." He'd repeat these words over and over throughout the day, and eventually convinced himself that he was. Years later, when he won the Olympic gold medal, he credited his ability to mentally convince himself first by saying "I am"—then backing up his words with action.

The take-away points from this example are that, for anything that you want to accomplish, you must first see it in your mind. You must tell yourself that:

- "I am the greatest businessman in the world."
- "I am the greatest mother or father that I can be."

- "I am the greatest athlete in my sport."
- "I am the greatest person I can be."

When you first begin to tell yourself these things, they may not seem right. They may seem like you're lying to yourself. Most of the time, you are! This brings us to the second take-away point from the example above: repetition!

If you truly want to be your best, repetitiously telling yourself that you *are* what you want to be is the only way to get there. Success does not happen randomly. Saying, "I am…" writing "I am…" and seeing yourself as you dream of being is the only way to get there. Again, it may seem far-fetched when you first start doing it. However, after a while, it becomes second nature. Before you know it, you'll have forced these sayings into your subconscious, until your mind actually believes them. Once you've convinced yourself that your dreams and goals are possible, then you'll be more prone to back up what you say and what you write with action.

The phrase "I am" will only work as a catalyst for achieving your goals if you back up your thoughts with action. If you've followed my advice and established goals that will force you to reach your potential, you cannot simply go through the motions to get there. You need to write it, say it, visualize it, and back it up with action. If Milt Campbell had told himself, "I am the greatest athlete in the world," but never worked to improve his strength, speed, endurance, and technique, do you think he would still have become a gold medalist? Most likely not! But because he repetitiously convinced himself that it was possible, and that he was the greatest athlete in the world, he was able to finally back up his words and thoughts with action and accomplish the impossible.

So, I want you to write down a list of all of the aspects of your life in which you wish to improve (be sure to add this list to your Motivational Binder). Then, I want you to formulate "I am" statements around each of them.

Examples:

- I am the best father in the world.
- I am the best at my profession in the country.
- I am the best athlete at my school.

For a sample of my personal "I am" list, visit www.unstoppablesuccess. com and use my list as your guide.

These are your dreams. These are your goals. Don't be afraid to start small and dream bigger as time goes on. At the same time, don't be afraid to aim for the moon immediately. If you want to be the best in the country, then don't write that you want to be the best in the state. If you want to be *your* best at something rather than *the* best, then write that instead. Once your list is in your Motivational Binder, be sure to review it every single day. Remember, none of these affirmations are set in stone. You can always upgrade your goals as you go. Write down your goals today in the "I am" format, then update them in the future if need be. But write down something today. Don't wait until tomorrow to figure out what you want. It's action that makes the difference. Do it right now!

Success Strategies

- The two most important words in your future success are "I am."
- Physical success begins in your mind.
- Through repetition in your thoughts and words, you can become the person you want to be.
- Visualize your goals, speak your goals, write your goals, and back up your thoughts and words with action.
- Start small if necessary and upgrade your goals as you go.

The next list that you will start to compile after completing your "I am" list is of....

The People You Will Meet

According to research, the two things in life that will shape who you become more than anything else are the people you meet and the books you read. Let's start by talking about the people you meet.

I do two things in order to maximize the effect of the people whom I meet, and I now suggest that you follow my lead. First, I want to make sure that I'm meeting the right people. Each year, I create a list of at least ten people I plan to meet in the next twelve months. I seek out people who are motivated in an area I'm looking to improve. I suggest that you go straight to the top. For example, if I'm looking to improve as an athlete, I try to meet and learn from the absolute best person I can find. If I want to improve in business, I look for those who have the absolute best businesses in my field. Once this list is complete, I place it in my Motivational Binder and review it each and every day until I have completed making the contacts. This process seems elementary, and really, it is. But are you doing it? You may have met one thousand different people last year, but how many of them did you *intentionally* pursue in order to soak up as much information from as possible?

When I look at my list of priorities and plan out my upcoming goals and areas of improvement, I then look for very specific people who can bring me closer to the level I desire. Once I find them, I get their phone numbers and call them to set up a lunch. Before the meeting, I make sure that I'm prepared. I research them and their business. I ask their friends about them, and I specifically ask them about achievements that they might not tell me about for fear of bragging. I write all of this information down and review it the night prior to the meeting.

At the meeting, I always open by letting them know that I have no hidden agendas. All I want is to learn a few things from them. Many times, I bring a gift to the meeting; such as a book their friends have told me they'd like, or something of that nature. If you intentionally go out of your way to track down motivated people who are successful at what they do, your expectations for yourself will start to rise immediately.

Each time I leave a meeting like this, I am energized, excited, and more motivated than ever to make my own dreams come true. Mainly, this is because I always come away thinking, "I can do that too!" The people I've sought out, just like those you'll seek and find, are just that—people! Learn how they think and what they do to be successful. Remember, there is no copyright on success. You too can follow in their footsteps!

The second action I take, which I now recommend to you, is to list of all of the people in my life who are the most important and influential. I also place this list in my Motivation Binder and review it each day. This list includes family members, friends, coworkers, former and current coaches, speakers that I've listened to, authors of books that I've read, and even many of the people whom I've actively sought out to learn from. Reading through the list and thinking about these people each and every morning reminds me of their impact on my life and forces me to recall things that I've learned from them. Again, if the people with which we associate are one of the two most influential sources in our lives, we want to make sure the lessons and love that we've gained from them are not forgotten.

Success Strategies

- Identify at least ten people you'd like to meet and learn from in the next twelve months.
- There is no copyright on success.
- What someone else can do, you can do also.
- List and review daily the most influential people in your life.
- After formal education, your two main sources of knowledge are the people you meet and the books you read.

So now that you have dealt with the people in your life, it's time to discuss....

The Books You Read

The second most important influence in your life next to the people you meet is the books that you read. Again, you can take steps to maximize this source of motivation and wisdom, just as you can maximize the positive influence of the people you meet. For my part, I take a two-step approach that's very similar to my approach to meeting people. I make a list of at least ten books that I want to read in the upcoming twelve months. I always end up exceeding this number, but I believe it is a great starting point. Again, I try to place books on my list that will help me in the various aspects of my life that I wish to improve. Each year I choose books on everything from relationships and business, to leadership, chiropractic, and health. I'll listen to many of the audio versions of these books to drive home the message and maximize my time. Let me point out to you, though, that this list of ten books is purely for motivational and educational purposes. It's absolutely great if you also like to read novels, but don't include them in the list of ten books that I want you to assemble unless you feel they'll inspire you in some significant way.

Once I've decided on ten books, I place them on my Christmas wish list. Any books that I do not receive for Christmas, I immediately look to buy before the New Year. Once I have them all in hand, I assemble them in order of priority and begin reading the first one, placing the other nine on hold and out of sight. I've found that focusing on reading only one book at a time is key to finishing it. Anytime that I've ever starting reading multiple books at once, I inevitably become more involved in one of them and place the other, partially finished books on hold. By the time I've finished the priority book, it's extremely hard to get myself to go back and continue the other ones. Reading one book at a time and having other books waiting for me that I will not allow myself to read until I'm finished with the book in hand gives me extra motivation to complete the book. I point this out to you because, year after year, statistics show that most people fail to actually finish the books that they start. Most books are just like this one in that, if you only read a part of what was written, you'll miss the entire premise of the book. As you remember from the Four Keys to Success, one major key to success is to *always finish what you start.*

My second action to maximize the effects of books I read, which I now suggest to you, is to write a full list of the influential books that you've read and place it in your Motivational Binder as well. I'm sure this sounds absurd to you, but please indulge me for a moment. Having spoken to several people who are also avid readers like me, I've found that nearly everyone has the same challenge that I have: we forget what we've read. For instance, whenever I'm reading a book about leadership, I feel that I'm able to put the concepts of the book into action each day. As I continue through the book, the skills I learn continue to improve in my life. However, if I finish that book and move on to a book about finance, my financial skills begin to improve, but my leadership skills decline because I'm no longer focused on that aspect of teaching. To be motivated for life, you need to be able to improve in multiple areas at once. This means that you need to be reminded at the onset of each new day of the lessons that you've learned from both the people you've met and the books you've read. I am by no means suggesting that you write a book report about each book that you've read; rather, just write enough to remind yourself of the premise of the book. For me, writing down the title of the book is enough. Quickly reviewing the titles of the books that I've read is an effective reminder to concentrate on implementing the lessons that I've learned, so I can use them to make *today* the best day ever. Reading through this list each day takes no more than a minute or two, but ensures that I'll continue to apply what I've learned without regressing. Again, let me point out to you that the sole purpose of writing down books you want read, as well as reviewing books you have read each day, is to maximize their effect. For my part, I don't trust myself to implement what I've learned unless I intentionally put myself in a position to be reminded of it. I want the reminders to help me excel at the tasks at hand *today.*

Success Strategies

- Successful people never stop learning.

- Identify at least ten books that you would like to read in the next twelve months.

- Always finish one book in its entirety before moving on to the next one.

- List and daily review the most influential books that you have read.

- Reviewing the books you have read will assure that you continue to implement what you have learned.

All of the previous lessons and information has been provided so that you can organize what I feel is the best tool that you will ever have in your motivational arsenal. It is what I refer to as the....

Chapter 14

THE MOTIVATIONAL SOLUTION

Repetition is the mother of skill. —*Anthony Robbins*

Now that you've learned to think like motivated people think and know what you want in your life, it's time to put it all together in a format that will allow you to get and stay internally motivated by your own vision. *All of the necessary forms are available for you to download for free at www.unstoppablesuccess.com.*

The Motivational Binder

As I stated at the onset of the book, all of the stories and suggestions that I have given you thus far will culminate into the Motivational Binder. The binder itself will contain, in my opinion, everything that you will need to *get* motivated and *stay* motivated in your life. The key here is that you must do what I suggest first, and that is you must review the forms in your Motivational Binder each and every day. That means on weekdays, on weekends, on workdays, on holidays, and even on vacation. You'll find that this takes very little time to complete, and even less time once you get use to reviewing your binder. Being motivated for life is something that requires daily attention. Don't get to this point in the book and say, "Yeah, I already know that," and then *not* do what's necessary for success. This binder sums up most of what I'm trying to get you to do to achieve unstoppable success. If you've accepted the premise of my book, then you *must* follow the steps that I'll lay out to complete your Motivational Binder, and you *must* review the binder at the beginning of each and every day. This is nonnegotiable!

Please remember that motivation doesn't just randomly "happen" on its own. People have often told me that I am one of the most motivated people they've ever met. While I take this as a compliment, they don't realize how hard I have to work to *keep* myself motivated. I wasn't just born with motivation; I have to work at it. As I've said before, I simply do the things that we all *know* that we should do to keep myself excited about achieving my purpose and reaching my goals. I've worked to connect the dots between *knowing* and *doing* to stay on task, and have done so by repetitively reviewing where I want my life to go.

Here's an example of why repetition is such an important tool, and one that I use all of the time. If you're married, you will certainly relate to my plight. Having been married for several years now, I know that my wife really appreciates it if I do certain things around the house. At the same time, if I don't complete those tasks, she gets the feeling that I'm not helping or don't care about the house and all of the work that she does. One particular task that she appreciates the most is doing the laundry.

Here's how the cycle used to go during the first few years of my marriage. It would begin with my wife feeling overwhelmed by everything that she had to do to keep our apartment or house in order. She would proceed to explain to me the importance of keeping up with my share of the household chores, which included helping with the laundry. I would then immediately get caught up with the laundry, and would stay on top of it for the next several days. Anytime that I began to assist with the laundry, my life got a whole lot better. My wife was always very appreciative, and went above and beyond to make sure that I knew it. However, as time went by, I'd help less and less with the laundry, until the whole cycle started again. I knew that she wanted it done, I knew how much better things were for me when I provided the assistance, and it really was not hard at all to do. I simply let it slip from my daily routine and forgot about it. In other words, I didn't *do* what I *knew* I should. After completing this cycle several times, I finally put a stopgap in place: I wrote myself a daily reminder to "help with the laundry." Life got better, and stayed better!

The same is true of your goals. If you want a motivated life, you need to have a daily list of reminders of what you have learned, where you are going, and the priorities and virtues that you plan to use today to help you get there. If you never write down what you've learned from people and books, then you'll never remember to implement as many of those lessons as possible each day. If you never write down your list of priorities in life, you'll never stick to them and will be easily distracted. If you never write your list of daily reminders, you'll never follow your own virtues. If you never review your goals, you'll never remember where you are going, and therefore won't make the daily decisions to get there.

That said, even if you complete all of the forms and place them in your Motivational Binder, you won't achieve the motivated life you want if you don't review them each and every day. So do yourself a favor: just follow the steps to complete the binder, and then put it in a place where you'll be forced to review it each and every morning before beginning your day.

As a physician, I am frequently asked about which exercise routine is the best. My response is, "The one that you do every day." I am also asked which diet is the best. My response is, "The one you follow each and every day." These are often given as tongue-in-cheek answers, but they are the truth. Of course, there are differences among the various exercise and diet programs available, and some of them are more helpful than others. But without consistency, none of them will work. Consistency has a way of making nearly everything work better. Give me any of the recommended exercise programs or diet plans, add consistency, and you will see some kind of results. The importance of consistency cannot be overstated. It is crucial to a motivated life.

As you complete the lists in this book, you'll find that I leave very little to chance, especially when it comes to rules to live by. I state each rule in three different ways: in the first person singular, in the second person, and in the third person. For example, if I'm reminding myself to be unstoppable, I write one page that states, "I am unstoppable," one page that states, "Be unstoppable," and one page that states, "Mike Mason is unstoppable." I review all three versions each morning. I originally started by stating the rules in only one form, but as time went on, I found more conviction in writing and reviewing them in multiple formats. Don't think too much about it, just do it!

Also, please make sure that you complete these forms immediately and place them in your binder. If you'd like to use my own personal forms as a guide, visit the web site www.unstoppablesuccess.com and download them for free. But use them only as a guide. Your purpose in life, your goals, and your rules to live by will be different than mine. Remember that they do not have to be perfected before you start reviewing them each morning. As I still frequently do, you'll find that you'll modify and update these forms as your life progresses. There is absolutely nothing wrong with this. It *would* be wrong to wait until you have everything absolutely right before beginning this process. Do your best with what you have right now, and modify the forms as you go. Also, remember that you can always add more to this Motivational Binder if you so desire. This is your motivational tool, and there are no limits to what you can do with it. The forms that I've listed below represent what I believe to be the essential guides to the life of your dreams.

The forms that you will use are as follows:

- **Life Purpose Statement.** As you've seen throughout the course of this book, I consider this to be the most important aspect of your binder and potentially the most motivating factor of your life. If you are like me, this will require multiple drafts before it is perfected. Write it today and perfect it later.

- **Personal Priorities.** I want you to write your priorities in life, as you *want* them to be, not necessarily as they currently are. This list of priorities, when reviewed daily, will force you to keep first things first in your life.

- **Daily Rules to Live By.** All of your daily rules are included here. Whether you list the Ten Commandments, words of wisdom from your parents, lessons learned throughout your life, or a combination, this list is one that will help you *do* the things you *know* you should by reminding you of how you want to live.

- **"I Am" Reminders.** This list is also derived from where you see yourself in the future, and not necessarily where you are at currently. If you dream big and write large "I am" goals, they'll seem funny and unimaginable the first few times you go through them. But by repetitively reviewing them each day, you'll start to see yourself as the person you want to be, and consequently will do what the person you want to be *would* do in all situations. Once you have these "I am" reminders ingrained into your subconscious, you'll begin to "bet on yourself" as I want you to.

- **Third-Person Reminders.** Occasionally I find myself looking from the outside in. Because of this, I decided to write my daily rules to live by as if I were looking at myself from the outside. This may be superfluous, but that's okay. By writing out your rules in this format, I feel that you will ensure that, regardless of your perspective on daily situations and challenges, you'll live by your rules. If you imagine the potential responses to your decisions from another person's perspective, you'll find you often make a different decision.

- **"Be, Do and Have."** We've discussed creating lists of both one- and five-year goals in-depth. In addition to placing this form in the Motivational Binder, I also recommend that you laminate several copies and post them in places where you'll see them through your day. Be it at school, at work, in the kitchen, in the bathroom, or in your car, reviewing your goals many times per day can only bring you closer to achieving your dreams. Make sure that you include exact end dates for completing your goals.

- **Books to Read and People to Meet:** As we've discussed, I recommend that you list at least ten to fifteen books and people. If you choose to have more, that's absolutely great. Regardless, make sure that you also include an exact end date on this list of goals.

- **Influential People and Books in Your Life.** I am not suggesting that you list every single person you know, but rather those whom you view as the most important in your life. People you want to emulate, people who have influenced you, former or current coaches, and family members are a few examples of individuals to list. The same goes for books that you've read. If you are an avid reader, you do not have to list every book if you don't want to, but rather the most important ones. Additionally, if there are any specific lessons you've learned from these books that you want to be reminded of, list them alongside the book title.

Success Strategies

- Visit www.unstoppablesuccess.com to download your Motivational Binder forms. Simply click on:" Free Gift" and download all of the forms for free. You also have free access to my own personal Motivational Binder to use as a guide for creating your own.

- Complete the forms and place them in your Motivational Binder today. You can alter them, as you go, so don't wait for them to be perfect before you start to review them.

- Review your Motivational Binder each and every day and watch your dreams become reality.

- Consistency has a way of making everything work better.

- Your Motivational Binder will become your own personal blueprint for unstoppable success.

Once you've completed this binder, remember that your new-motivated life should not end there. In addition to your Motivational Binder, you must continue to....

Surround Yourself with Success

As I pointed out earlier, you go where you look. If you want to be motivated for life, then you need to look for motivation. It's there, but you have to be looking for it.

To prove my point, I once followed a friend's advice and started writing down some of the funny things that happen every day at my job. At that point, I probably ran into a funny story only about once or twice a month. I decided that I'd buy a small notebook and carry it with me in my back pocket throughout the workday. In it, I would write down every funny story that came my way (though, obviously, I never wrote down names). You'd be amazed how many funny stories began to appear. I'm sure that these funny events had always been there, but because I was not necessarily looking for them, I didn't notice them. Following the success of the funny stories that found their way into my notebook, I decided to do the same with motivational stories and events. Surprisingly enough, what happened was exactly the same. I began to find everything motivational. One motivating thing after another appeared in front of me. The same will happen for you. We are all surrounded by potential inspiration and motivation, but we have to look for it and see it in others.

At the same time, I have *intentionally* surrounded myself with motivation everywhere I look. The following are some examples of actions and habits that keep me motivated. I recommend that you *do* the same:

- Complete your Motivational Binder and keep it in a place where you will read it every morning.
- Listen to motivational music, as you get ready for your day.

- Keep motivational audios in your car that you listen to when driving to and from work.

- Write your Purpose Statement on a note card, keep it in your wallet, and review it multiple times per day.

- Write down your goals, laminate the papers, and hang the pages in the places that you'll see the most (e.g., the refrigerator, the bathroom, the inside of your bathroom cabinet, in your car, etc.)

- Keep a book of motivational quotes nearby and focus on one quote per day. If you work at an office with other employees, read them a "quote of the day" or copy down motivational quotes on Post-its and give them out each day.

- Intentionally surround yourself with motivated people.

- Seek out people who are even more motivated than you.

- See every challenge in your life and in the lives of others as chances to motivate them or yourself to succeed.

- Read motivational books.

- Give motivational books and items to others in need.

- Watch motivational movies and documentaries.

- Surround yourself with framed pictures and quotes that are motivational.

- Find motivational seminars and attend them.

- Motivate others by always being excited when they achieve their goals.

- Motivate yourself and others by smiling through your day.

In addition to the Motivational Binder, I recommend taking many other actions to consistently maintain a motivated attitude. For example, "vision boarding" is another effective motivational tool. Made popular by the best-selling book *The Secret*, vision-boarding web sites have popped up everywhere on the Internet. They are another means of putting your life goals and vision in a graphic format, through computer programs that steer you toward defining various goals for your life. I'm a huge fan of vision boarding. However, if you choose to create a vision board, remember that it is in addition to, and does not replace, your Motivational Binder.

Whatever you might decide to do, just make sure that you *intentionally* surround yourself with reminders of where you're going and your ability to be motivated for life at this very moment.

Success Strategies

- You are surrounded by inspiration if you look for it.
- Keep your Purpose Statement with you and review it throughout your day.
- Place lists of your ultimate goals and dreams in places where you will see them throughout your day.
- Read a motivational quote each morning and concentrate on it throughout your day.
- Fill your day with motivational music, motivational books, motivational audio courses, motivational seminars, and motivational movies.

When doing so, you will be much more qualified to quickly conquer any and all of your failures and setbacks, and you'll be ready to move to....

Chapter 15

SUCCESS AND BEYOND

I know God won't give me anything I can't handle;
I just wish he didn't trust me so much. —Mother Theresa

O f all of the various aspects of my athletic career, I attribute the majority of my success to a sole quality: I learned from my mistakes. Even when I was very young, I was very deliberate in my approach to the sport. Every time I gave up a point, I quickly looked for a solution with the help of teammates and coaches so that it wouldn't happen again. Even in practice, if I gave up a point (which was often), I would write down what I needed to work on the following day so that I could correct the mistake. Once I found the solution, I would repeat the move over and over until it became a reaction. In competition, I learned that most people did not do this. Early in my career, I could usually play the same tricks over and over on the same person in multiple matches. However, as the competition stage grew and the competitors got better, I began to notice that they all followed this same rule. The best competition for me was the one in which my opponent and I had both learned from our mistakes and each had to play a better game the next time we met. But don't forget that in order to get better, first we had to *make mistakes*.

Failure and Setbacks

If there's anything that I'm qualified to write about, it's mistakes. I've experienced setbacks and failures more times than you can imagine, and more times than I would actually care to admit. Small failures and large, I've had them all. Failures in athletics, in coaching, in school, in business, in finance, in relationships, and in life. However, I've always viewed failure as temporary. When you keep your eye on the bigger picture, you begin to realize that failure isn't failure at all. I have always used failure to my advantage. What I mean is that I focus first on finding a solution and second on making sure that I never repeat the same mistake. When you're motivated for life, you'll learn from every mistake and use that knowledge to propel you to greater heights.

Look at any sport, and you'll find the greatest athletes will always recover from and correct their mistakes. They all stick to the saying "Fool me once, shame on you. Fool me twice, shame on me." I've come to realize that the best of the best in any sport or line of work not only correct their mistakes, but do so more effectively and quickly than everyone else. You'll never see a motivated person accept failure as anything more than temporary. Motivated people quickly find a solution and begin moving forward again, knowing that there is a reason for everything.

I've never claimed to be an extraordinary athlete by any stretch of the imagination. However, I do believe that I reached my full potential while competing, and because of that, I was able to accomplish some extraordinary things. One such accomplishment was making it into the NCAA Division I national semifinals, which is similar to the Final Four in basketball. Every former athlete has a "would have, could have, should have" story, and mine happened to occur in that particular match. Unfortunately, I found myself on the losing side of a controversial call that cost me the match and my ultimate athletic dream of becoming an NCAA champion. I went into that tournament and that match *knowing* that I was going to win. I can honestly say that it never crossed my mind that losing was a possibility. Before I go on, let me point out that feeling certain of success is wonderful, and something you'll experience yourself if you follow the recommendations that I've given you. Anyway, the night of that loss was the longest of my life. To most people, the loss would have been nothing major, especially after making it all the way to the "Final Four." But for me, it was everything. As I sat by my bed the entire night, I reflected on my preparation and concluded that I could not have possibly done anything more to prepare myself for that moment. Then I thought about some of the past athletes whom I had met, read about, and seen on television. I recalled so many people who had ended their career on a loss and had held on to that pain for years after. Then I remembered my purpose. My purpose for achieving my goals was to give all of the glory to God and to show my family, friends, and teammates that anything was possible, even for a mediocre athlete from a small town in West Virginia like me. I even carried with me my favorite Bible verse; "I raised you up for this very purpose, that I might display my power in you" (Romans 9:17). I pondered that quote for hours. Was it possible that I could still achieve my purpose without winning? Absolutely! I competed my way through two matches the following day en route to a third-place finish. I'd always believed that God's power would be displayed through me as I won the title, but his plan was for me was to have his power revealed by giving me the strength to recover. This is how I see failure now, as a means to show strength in your recovery. Following the conclusion of the tournament, I once again recalled all of those athletes who have never let go of their "story," and decided that I would not be one of them. While I was undoubtedly devastated by falling short of my goal, because I had a purpose greater than the achievement of any athletic title, I was able to move forward and use the event as a learning experience to better prepare me for coaching, for business, and for life.

In business, I've been successful because I condensed twenty years' worth of mistakes into my first few years. I made mistakes in marketing, in staffing, in managing, and in every other aspect of the business. But just as I'm suggesting to you, I learned from every single mistake and continued to improve so that my missteps were not repeated. I've learned from other successful people both in and outside of my field that you must be willing to get back up when you're knocked down and do a better job today than you did yesterday. The fun part in my business failures is that they've helped me correct specific areas much more quickly than I could have if I'd never made an error.

When I've talked to the business owners and entrepreneurs I've met in various coaching programs, I've found that nearly all of them, especially the most successful ones, have lost it all or have been in danger of losing it all at one point or another before they made it big. This is literally the case with every millionaire that I've ever met. But they've all used their failures to bring them to a higher level of productivity and success. Even people like Anthony Robbins, who hit rock bottom and felt hopeless before he became one of the world's leading life coaches, have had to overcome setbacks. Likewise, business coach, entrepreneur, and author of one of my favorite business books, *The E-Myth*, Michael Gerber writes about having to overcome his own financial troubles while running a business that teaches other people how to run *their* businesses. Can you imagine dealing with that issue? Again, he was struggling to run a worldwide business that coaches other people on how to run *their* businesses. How ironic it would have been for him to fail! But while most people would have downsized due to the stress involved, he used the challenges to motivate him to make his company one of the largest business education programs in the world.

Because I have a big life, I get big lessons. —Oprah Winfrey

No person is above problems. If you turn on the news tonight, you'll undoubtedly see a new celebrity or athlete scandal. We all look at their mistakes and immediately make judgments about their guilt or innocence. Most of the time, they're guilty of whatever is alleged. But does this make them bad people? Not necessarily. If they were not famous and not extraordinary at what they did, many of their mistakes would blend in with all of the mistakes that you and I make on a daily basis. However, because they are special, the media blows their problems out of proportion. The ones that are truly motivated for life correct their mistakes, make the necessary changes to ensure that they do not occur again, then use those mistakes to propel them forward in their careers. I point this out because, as you stretch your imagination and begin to move up the ladder of success, you will by no means be exempt from failures and setbacks. If anything, the failures get bigger and the setbacks seem more significant. The key is to maintain the same level of motivation and to have the same conviction in achieving success that you did in the easier stages of life. If you're sincerely working to correct your mistakes at *every* level of success, and if you are reviewing your Motivational Binder on a daily basis, then there is no obstacle that you cannot overcome.

Every failure carries with it an equal or greater benefit. —Napoleon Hill

Even financial losses are not necessarily losses at all. As one of my coaches continually points out to all of the people who complain about having "lost" money in the stock market, you didn't actually "lose" money unless you sold. You can see it as a loss, or you can see it as a possibility for future growth. How you view failure will affect how you handle virtually every aspect of your life. If you experience a financial loss in the stock market and conclude that people can't make money in the stock market, you're missing a huge opportunity. If you or someone you know ever made a bad real estate deal, and you conclude that people can't make money in real estate, you're missing a huge opportunity. If you've ever had a relationship go bad and concluded that you can never trust anyone, you're missing a huge opportunity. When you can learn and truly accept that every failure is temporary, and every temporary failure carries with it "an equal or greater benefit," as Napoleon Hill suggested, you'll be well on your way to living a motivated life.

It is dismissive to think that you can accomplish any large goal or achieve any worthwhile purpose unscathed. You need to become accustomed to dealing with setbacks and smiling your way through them. According to author Jeffrey Gitomer, when you can mentally work your way through any problem or failure in two minutes or less, you have achieved the kind of attitude that will lead to a motivated life.[6]

---

6   Jeffrey Gitomer, *Little Gold Book of YES! Attitude*, 192–193.

Success Strategies

- Failures and setbacks are necessary for progress.

- Successful people have learned to make and correct more mistakes in a shorter period of time.

- Every failure should be viewed as temporary.

- A strong purpose behind your actions will push you through any challenge.

- Successful people know that every problem is accompanied by a bigger opportunity.

I believe that this kind of attitude about mistakes and failures is easily attainable when you….

Love to be Your Best

Nothing great was ever achieved without enthusiasm. —John Maxwell

As I already mentioned, as a high school athlete, I experienced an unfortunate loss at a very bad time, during the high school state finals. The pain I felt was enormous. For many athletes, falling short of a goal like this is very similar to dealing with a death. Obviously, it's just a sport and not a life, but try explaining that to a fourteen-year-old. It's the death of a dream. Your chance is over. I used the pain of that loss to drive me through the following 365 days, until I could overcome that loss and become a state champion. In the process, I learned a lesson that's also taught in Anthony Robbins's books. People are driven by two things and two things only: pleasure and pain. According to Anthony Robbins, people will do more to avoid pain than they will to gain pleasure. I learned that his premise, at least in my experience, certainly held true. I would have done anything to avoid feeling defeated ever again. And because of that, I was driven to push myself even harder to reach the top. However, the true lesson that I learned is that, while you may do more to avoid pain than to gain pleasure, avoiding pain isn't fun at all. The following year after that loss brought me to a higher level of success, but at times, it felt like a chore because I was working to avoid future pain. Only when I changed my thinking and became excited about the possibilities did striving to be the best become more fun. I used that lesson to drive me not only through the remainder of my athletic career, but also in the classroom, as a coach, and eventually in business.

Hines Ward of the Pittsburgh Steelers is one of my favorite sports examples of this principle. Anytime he's caught on camera during a game, he's always smiling. You can tell how excited he is just to be out there on the field. He likes to play—and he loves to win! It's impossible to say what's actually motivating him internally to be one of the best players in the NFL, but at least externally, it's all about enjoying being his best.

Likewise, multiple interviews with Donald Trump have revealed that his fierce drive is based on his love of being number one. In all of those interviews, I've never heard him say anything about fear. Even when he had to rebuild his empire several years ago, he declared that his drive was to "be the best." Maybe he was also driven to avoid the pain of the loss that he had experienced, but it is evident that he loves to succeed and isn't only driven by the avoidance of pain.

As you review the goals that you've set for your motivated life, I want you to begin to get excited about the *feeling* of achieving the life that you want. Since you can't achieve your lofty goals in a single day, you need to start recognizing and celebrating the small victories along the way. Anytime that I can do something better today than I did yesterday, I love it! I've learned to both notice and find immense joy in knowing that I did my best, even if the end result doesn't necessarily reveal a change. Growth is growth in any way, shape, or form. I love to improve. When you can find joy in knowing that you did your best, great results will soon follow. As you learned in the section "Breaking It Down," the smaller goals along the path to the larger goal must be celebrated not only when they are accomplished, but also with each step in the right direction.

I've personally used this principle most often in my business. As the business continues to grow, I set up personal rewards for myself with each minor sign of growth along the way. I've used dinners, trips, watches, and even golf clubs as rewards for myself. Partly because of this, I now love to hit my goals! As you should be learning by this point in the book, I've set up routine, predictable events in each day of my life to keep me motivated to get everything out of life that I can and to give everything that I have to it. These suggestions have worked for me, and they will work for you when you *act* on them.

Success Strategies

- Enthusiasm is a catalyst to unstoppable success.
- Focus on the feeling you will have when you accomplish your goals and dreams.
- Recognize and celebrate the small victories along your journey.
- Taking joy in knowing that you did your best is soon followed by extraordinary results.
- Establish your rewards for achieving each goal and use the reward to motivate you.

Just remember that you don't have all the time in the world. The clock is already ticking. And just as this book is coming to an end, all of our lives are approaching an end as well. The key is….

Ending with Purpose

My pastor once told a story about a very wealthy man in the community who unexpectedly passed away. People in the church began to speculate about the amount of money, jewelry, real estate, and intangibles that he must have left to the church and remaining family members. Several of his friends asked around, trying to find out how much the man was worth, and they found out the pastor had been named as the executor of the will. Following the funeral, one man quietly approached the pastor and said, "I promise that we won't spread the word too far, but I and some of his other friends were wondering if you could tell us how much he left behind."

The preacher looked at him like a father at a child and replied, "He left it all, and so will we."

Remember that being motivated for life will lead you to achieve all of your goals. There's nothing wrong with having goals about acquiring material possessions. But I want to reiterate that you must have a purpose for acquiring those things that is centered around other people. Your purpose is paramount in the process of living a motivated life. Of all of the lessons and recommendations that I have given you in this book, I consider the Purpose Statement to be the most important. Recite it to yourself throughout the day. Read it in your Motivational Binder every day. Write it in places where you'll be able to read it throughout your day. Start living like a person with a purpose in everything that you do.

Now you know these things. You will be blessed if you do them.
—John 13:17

Success Strategies

- Unstoppable success only occurs when you back up your thoughts with action.

- Now is the best time you will ever have to start living the life that you want.

- Your Purpose Statement is the most powerful motivational tool that you will ever establish.

- Possessions are temporary, but the person you become will always remain.

- When you become unstoppable, you give those around you permission to elevate their lives as well.

If at the beginning of this book, you were not yet successful, the insight given to you in these lessons will give you the mindset you need to be motivated for life. If you were already successful, then hopefully this book forced you to expand your expectations and dream bigger than you ever have before. *Now is the time to connect the dots between knowing and doing.* You know what to do, now do it! Life is too short not to. Countless people pass away each day who have always known what they *could* have done and what they *should* have done, yet who lacked the motivation to put their knowledge into action. Life is filled with unmotivated people. You won't be one of them.

AFTERWORD

You did then what you knew to do, and when you knew better,
you did better. —Maya Angelou

As a coach and motivator, I have often said:

Show me a person with extraordinary potential that lacks
motivation, and I will show you a waste of talent. Show me a
person with ordinary potential who has motivation, and I will
show you success. And in those special cases where you combine
extraordinary potential with extraordinary motivation, that person
becomes unstoppable. My goal for you is to become unstoppable!

I implore you to follow the advice that I've given you in this book. As
I stated at the onset of our journey together, I've done every single
thing that I propose. I'm convinced that my success up to this point
has been possible because of the information that I've shared, and I'm
also convinced that if I continue to follow these recommendations, I'll
get even closer to my own potential in the future. This information has
cost me years of trial and error, hundreds of thousands of dollars, and a
lifetime of accumulating as much knowledge as possible from some of the
most successful and motivated people in the world. I sincerely appreciate
you allowing me to help you start your quest for being motivated for life.
Helping you achieve your potential is part of my own purpose in life. So
by reaching your own potential, you're not only helping yourself achieve

your own purpose, but you're also helping me achieve mine as well. If you were ever asked, "What would you *do* if you won the lottery?" I hope that you can respond as I do:

"I feel like I've already won and *I'm doing it!*"

If I can be of any assistance to you along the way, please don't hesitate to contact me at www.unstoppablesuccess.com. I love nothing more in life than helping other people reach their dreams. My promise to you is that I will always be a source of encouragement for you and will continue to demand the most out of myself in order to bring the best possible motivation to you for your life.

Unstoppable success is as simple as doing the things necessary to be better today than you were yesterday, with the intention of becoming better tomorrow than you were today. —Mike Mason

ABOUT THE AUTHOR

 **Dr. Mike Mason** is the clinic director of The Chiropractic Care Center, PLLC, where he has helped thousands of patients get well and stay well through natural healthcare. He is also the founder of Unstoppable Business Consulting, a seminar and coaching program geared towards motivating and educating both current and future business owners. He can be reached directly at: www.unstoppablesuccess.com where he and his team of professionals are committed to helping you *grow your business and expand your life*.

A former Division 1 All American athlete and high school wrestling coach, Mike Mason is an expert at maintaining and adapting motivation. He transferred his competitive sports drive to the academic arena and later to the financial and business world. He lectures on health and motivation to sports and business groups. He resides in Bridgeport, West Virginia with his wife Natalie and their children, Rachel and Tyler.

ADDITIONAL RESOURCES

Galie, Anthony. *Take Control of Your Subconscious Mind.* Melbourne Beach: Cornerstone Press, 2000.

Gerber, Michael. *The E-Myth Revisited.* New York: HarperCollins, 1995.

Gitomer, Jeffrey. *Little Gold Book of YES! Attitude.* Upper Saddle River, NJ: FT Press, 2007.

Hill, Napoleon. *Grow Rich! With Peace of Mind.* New York: Penguin Group, 2007.

Langemeier, Loral. *The Millionaire Maker.* New York: McGraw-Hill, 2006.

Maxwell, John. *The 360 Degree Leader.* Nashville: Thomas Nelson, 2005.

Robbins, Anthony. *Awaken the Giant Within.* New York: Free Press, 1991.

Waitzkin, Josh. *The Art of Learning.* New York: Free Press, 2007.

Warren, Rick. *The Purpose Driven Life.* Grand Rapids: Zondervan, 2002.

Ferriss, Timothy. *The 4-Hour Workweek.* New York: Crown Publishing Group, 2007.

BUY A SHARE OF THE FUTURE IN YOUR COMMUNITY

These certificates make great holiday, graduation and birthday gifts that can be personalized with the recipient's name. The cost of one S.H.A.R.E. or one square foot is $54.17. The personalized certificate is suitable for framing and will state the number of shares purchased and the amount of each share, as well as the recipient's name. The home that you participate in "building" will last for many years and will continue to grow in value.

Here is a sample SHARE certificate:

YES, I WOULD LIKE TO HELP!

I support the work that Habitat for Humanity does and I want to be part of the excitement! As a donor, I will receive periodic updates on your construction activities but, more importantly, I know my gift will help a family in our community realize the dream of homeownership. **I would like to SHARE in your efforts against substandard housing in my community!** *(Please print below)*

PLEASE SEND ME _____ SHARES at $54.17 EACH = $ $_____

In Honor Of: _____

Occasion: (Circle One)   HOLIDAY   BIRTHDAY   ANNIVERSARY

      OTHER: _____

Address of Recipient: _____

Gift From: _____ *Donor Address:* _____

Donor Email: _____

I AM ENCLOSING A CHECK FOR $ $_____ PAYABLE TO HABITAT FOR HUMANITY OR PLEASE CHARGE MY VISA OR MASTERCARD *(CIRCLE ONE)*

Card Number _____ Expiration Date: _____

Name as it appears on Credit Card _____ Charge Amount $ _____

Signature _____

Billing Address _____

Telephone # Day _____ Eve _____

PLEASE NOTE: Your contribution is tax-deductible to the fullest extent allowed by law.
Habitat for Humanity • P.O. Box 1443 • Newport News, VA 23601 • 757-596-5553
www.HelpHabitatforHumanity.org

Printed in the USA
CPSIA information can be obtained
at www.ICGtesting.com
JSHW082208140824
68134JS00014B/496